Chasing Love
(BOOK 1: LOVE GAMES SERIES)

Laura Pinks

I hope you enjoy reading this as much as I enjoyed writing it.

love
Laura Pinks

LAURA PINKS

Copyright © 2015 Laura Pinks

All rights reserved.

ISBN:
ISBN-13: 978-1519669216
ISBN-10: 1519669216

DEDICATION

I dedicate this book to the younger me who always wanted to be a writer but never believed in herself enough to do anything about it. This one's for you girl.

ACKNOWLEDGMENTS

Wow, I can't believe I am actually at this stage now. After almost a whole year of working on this I am now publishing which is scary as hell.

*

Firstly I want to thank my little boy Charlie for napping so beautifully this past year. It gave me those couple of hours each day to plan, write and edit this story.

*

I have to thank my husband for being patient with me and putting up with me being glued to my laptop (and also helping me to buy the laptop too) He has even played a part in the editing process having read the story and done a round of edits on it, without him I would've missed some glaring mistakes.

*

I have to thank my Beta reader Lauren Greene who also played a huge part in the development of the story and gave me loads of advice to really make the story shine. She is a fellow author so highly recommend you guys reading her stuff.

*

Another author who I couldn't have done this without is the fabulous Beth Ashworth. With 3 titles already under her belt and a fourth on the way she was able to guide me through the times when I was completely clueless and about to give up. I will be forever grateful for your help throughout this weird and wonderful journey to becoming an author. Her work is a must read!

*

I need to give a big shout out to Sarah at Sprinkles on Top Studios who designed my cover. I hope you can agree she did a fantastic job and made the whole process so easy, especially for a newbie like me.

*

I couldn't write my acknowledgements without mentioning the 10 Minute Novelists. This fantastic, inspiring group of people have kept me going throughout the whole process. I have made some great friends and simply love being part of the 10MN family.

CHAPTER 1

"Well that's another satisfied customer" Libby beamed at Jane. Her and Jane had been friends for as long as she could remember. They'd lived together since university and when she'd had trouble finding work, Jane immediately offered her the assistant position in her dating agency. Libby, fun loving and fiery, was always excitable when she heard that a match they'd made had moved past a few dates and was getting serious. The truth was, Jane hadn't failed to make a perfect match in the last 5 years! Still, she thought it sweet that her best friend cared so much about her work. Hoping one day to expand the business to be able to get Libby involved in more than just organising her diary. Even though the business was booming, that day still seemed a little way off, as did her own chance of finding a serious relationship for that matter.

"Who have you heard from this time Hun?" Jane asked casually, having learnt to stem the excitement of yet another job well done so as not to seem conceited.

"Claire and Michael, they've emailed in to say that they have just booked their first holiday together and couldn't be happier. Don't you just love how they keep in touch with us even after months of dating. You really are a great match maker!"

"That's why I set up Love Games, you know I've always been good at getting people together. Look at you and Jamie how many years are we up to now? Oh and what's my schedule for the rest of the day?"

"10 and still going strong. Let me see, ahh you have a meeting with Joanna over lunch to set up her initial profile, good luck with that one; then you have a couple of hours free before your 3.30 with Dean and then a 4.30 with a prospective client named Andrew. He didn't leave a last name though, seemed a bit cold on the phone like he didn't even want to be calling."

"No-one really wants to admit they need help finding someone Lib. Are you alright to man the office until after my first appointment?" She wanted nothing more than a quiet coffee in her favourite place before the dreaded lunch with Joanna. She had, admittedly, been shocked when Joanna contacted her office to set up a meeting. Having always wanted things done in a particular way; her way, Jane just couldn't comprehend how she was going to be able to cope with letting someone else find her a man. You couldn't even order her a coffee without getting something wrong. Something she had learnt very early on, what with Joanna being her mothers close friend.

"Sure thing, see you later."

She picked up her folders and briefcase and walked out into the crowded street below her little office. The sun was beating down on her and she decided to walk to the coffee shop rather than drive. London was a nightmare at the best of times but to be stuck in traffic on a hot day like today would be a foolish mistake to make. Plus the fresh air should help her gather her thoughts for what she believed would be her hardest client to date.

***

Andrew hung up the phone after finally giving in and calling Love Games. He hated to admit that his PA was right, he did need help finding someone he could trust and sadly this seemed like it was the only way. He didn't have trouble finding women. He just had issues finding the right women.

Being one of the most eligible bachelors in London meant he could happily have his pick of any of them, but it meant he attracted all the wrong ones. The ones that would sleep with him in a heart beat if they saw a flash of Chanel or Gucci coming their way, but he was at that point in his life where he wanted more than just sex and lavish nights out. So how was he supposed to find a wife when he was always concerned what they really wanted, to marry him or his bank account?

No, this was the only way he could have a good chance of finding her. He'd been keeping an eye on Love Games since one of his clients had mentioned they'd heard rave reviews about the high success rates. He was surprised to hear that it had been founded by just one young woman and he admired her ability to make it work as well as it clearly did. He hoped she would be able to work her magic with him, but if he was being honest, he was dreading the whole thing. It somehow seemed below him and he was sure the girl he'd just spoken to on the phone could tell. He was glad he wasn't meeting with her.

***

Jane felt her phone vibrating in her briefcase as she walked along the street and struggled to find it. She considered just letting it go to voicemail. It was Ben, she had totally forgotten about him! He was the guy she'd met in the pub a few nights ago. He seemed nice enough and was handsome. Tall, with mousy hair and blue eyes and clearly looked after himself. She had a date with him that evening and it had somehow slipped her mind.

She had given up telling Libby about any new dates so as to avoid the Spanish Inquisition, either when she got home, or the morning after. Jane was a very good match maker, so much so that she centered her entire life around it. Yet her own love life left something to be desired and she used any way possible to avoid talking about it. Her recent dating history was nothing more than an embarrassing stream of one night stands. She just couldn't find that special person who took her breath away. You know, the guy that makes the whole world stand still in one magical moment of realisation that you simply cannot live without them.

No, sadly for that she was still searching. If she hadn't seen it happen with her clients she would swear it was all a lie made up by the film companies to force people to search for something that doesn't really exist, to the point that you just give up and settle for the one that annoys you the least.

Actually it is quite ironic how cynical Jane can be about love when her whole life revolves around it. Turning 29 really made her take stock of her life; seeing all her university friends settling down, getting married and even having children. Some were even on their second! Yet here she was, alone, and still living in a poxy 2 bedroom flat with her best friend.

"Hi Ben" She finally answered, whilst manoeuvring round various people window shopping in front of her.

"I was just checking you were still on for tonight? I hadn't heard from you so wanted to make sure you hadn't forgotten me."

"Sure! Tonight, of course, no I hadn't forgotten about it…. I have just been really busy this week." The truth was she hadn't actually given him a second thought after leaving the pub that night.

"That's good to hear. So is 8 o'clock good for you?"

"I will be at work until about 6pm so 8pm is actually perfect for me."

"I have made reservations but can't talk for long so I will text you the details this afternoon. Catch ya later babe."

"Yeah… me too. See you at 8." She didn't have butterflies, not a good start. In fact she thought she might not even be capable of having the feeling she helped so many others achieve. Still, she would keep trying to prove herself wrong, if she didn't then what would be the point of any of it? Her whole life would be a lie, and that was way too dramatic for her to even comprehend.

Without realising, she'd walked past the coffee shop and had to embarrassingly spin around and retrace her steps. Lost in her thoughts of the pained meeting she was sure to have with Joanna, and now having a date with a guy that, truthfully, she wasn't all that into, she wished she could just hide away somewhere warm and safe. There were some days where being an adult really sucked.

As soon as she walked into the shop she wanted the ground to swallow her up. She felt her face flush as she saw who was walking towards her. His grey pinstripe suit flattering his near perfect torso, which Jane knew was smooth and tanned. Although she couldn't see it, she had memorised the tight, pert bottom that followed him. It made her wonder how a man could look as good with his clothes on as he did with them off, better even in this case.

Her heart was pounding as she recalled the many, many nights where that man had been pressed on top of her. His breath in her ear getting heavier as they reached climax together. She hadn't thought it could ever get better than that. Well, apart from the total lack of commitment and knowing he was having these same evenings with numerous other women as well, but you can't have everything can you?!

William was heading straight towards her. It looked almost as if he couldn't see her, until he was just a few steps away. Then his eyes locked on to hers, making her loins burn and her mouth dry up.

"Well well well, hello there you. It's certainly been a while hasn't it?" William looked her up and down. A glimmer flashed in his eyes like he wanted to devour her. She didn't think it was possible to blush any more than she was doing right then and swore he was able to hear her heart thumping. Licking her lips, she took a deep breath and tried to compose herself before answering.

"William, what a pleasant surprise. It has been a while… but I see you have been keeping well." As soon as the words were out she wished she'd kept her mouth shut. The knowing smile meant he understood she'd been referring to his body. He knew how much she enjoyed it.

To make matters worse she now couldn't look him in the eye for fear of giving away her feelings. All she wanted to do was drag him into the restroom and have her way with him. Just remembering how it felt to be with a man made her realise how long it'd been since she had been with anyone physically. It had been months since she'd vowed to start looking for a serious relationship. The dry spell was starting to take it's toll.

"Just the usual gym routine, nothing new really. So how come I haven't seen you around? You always used to be in the White Hart, but since our last night together I haven't seen you once.... Have you been avoiding me?" He smiled again, knowing full well that she'd taken their 'break up' badly.

You couldn't actually call it a break up as they were never actually an official couple. They had the occasional meal together. What did it matter that the meal usually consisted of a takeaway pizza consumed naked in bed, it still counted as meal right? Most of the time though they would just meet up for sex. They would have it anywhere, everywhere and in any way they could.

Jane quickly stopped herself thinking about sex for fear she would start dry humping him there and then. Boy did she need an orgasm. Hell, she would even settle for a man just lying on top of her for a while to feel the pressure of another person on her. She recalled the moment she'd discovered she wasn't the only person that William was 'with'.

It turned out he had women everywhere. There were so many that sometimes he would shag someone different at breakfast, lunch and then dinner. It was like he just couldn't find someone to truly satisfy him, he always wanted more. Thankfully these thoughts gave her the boost she needed as she remembered what a sleaze he was.

"Absolutely not. Things have been busy at work! I even had to hire Libby to keep on top of it all."

"Well you don't look all that busy now, how about we jump in my car and....catch up?" He had that smouldering look in his eyes, the one he knew she wouldn't be able to resist. She now had a dilemma. She really should get things organised for this meeting with Joanna but boy did she need this.

She could make it clear that it would just be a one off. That he mustn't call her. Ever. As she was thinking this he traced a finger along her cheek and down to her lips where they hovered momentarily before gently brushing her bottom lip. His scent and sheer proximity made her dizzy. He however seemed unaffected by the electricity that was now coursing between them and simply leaned in to brush his lips gently against hers.

Her reaction was instant. Her lips responded as soon as contact was made. Starting off gently but growing more and more passionate as time went on; the more they kissed the more she wanted. He suddenly pulled away leaving her panting, wanting more. Her lips swollen from the passionate embrace they were no longer used to receiving. He smiled and motioned to the door. Like some obedient puppy she silently followed him through, knowing full well she was going against everything she actually wanted. To her this was a necessity, she had to get it out of her system so she could move on.

He led her a little way down the road and opened his car door. She slid in thankful she'd opted for a pencil skirt that morning. It wasn't until he was close beside her that she realised they were in the back. He'd barely closed the door before he was on top of her, kissing her passionately once again. His hands unbuttoning her blouse and caressing her breasts, tweaking her nipples through her satin bra which sent her into overdrive She greedily pulled open his shirt and wrenched herself away from the kiss to admire the body underneath it.

Once she'd had her fill of his chest she moved south, unzipping his perfectly fitted trousers. He took the hint and slid a hand up her skirt, massaging her folds, knowing exactly how to get her to the point of deliriousness. Slowly teasing her panties down before eagerly entering one finger inside her.

She was ridiculously wet, it was borderline embarrassing. Watching him as he pulled his slicked fingers in and out of her she knew she had to have all of him. Hitching her skirt up as she straddled him. Hovering her sex over his cock before expertly guiding him inside her. Slowly at first so she could relish in the full feeling she had missed. It had been too long so she wanted to make the most of this moment. She didn't know when it would be happening again and it sure wouldn't be with him.

He groaned loudly, which only encouraged her. She was like a woman possessed. Gyrating her hips, she rode him to the point where neither could take anymore. Together they reached the glorious point of climax. Her body shuddered around him as she felt the jolts of his ejaculation deep inside her. She wasn't sure at what point he'd slid on a condom, but was thankful he had been prepared. She really didn't have time to find a chemist today.

Trying to calm her breathing as she slid off him onto the back seat, she tried to compose herself and began rearranging her clothes. She didn't know what to say to him so made the simple task of re-buttoning her blouse take as long as she could before finally looking in his direction. He was staring at her as if attempting to read her thoughts.

"I have missed *you*." He said it in such an odd way, she knew he meant he'd missed her body and not her intellectual wit. This thought brought her back to reality instantly, and despite the ability to make her loose her mind when he touched her, he was nothing more than a whore and this would never change. Feeling annoyed with herself, she started picking up her files and located her briefcase which had been discarded during the brief but oh so satisfying encounter. She coughed to clear her throat.

"Well it was nice catching up with you, but I really must get on." She reached out for the handle but something made her look back round.

He was just sitting there smiling at her, well it was more of a smirk really, his eyes narrowed, but he didn't say a word.

"Well I really must be going. So...I'm going to leave now ok?" She wasn't sure what more she needed to say, she couldn't understand why William wasn't saying anything. She opened the door and started to get out when he finally spoke,

"Good to see you Jane, don't be a stranger" Winking at her as she slammed the door in his smug face.

What had she done? Had she really just gone back on everything she wanted for one stupid moment of passion? She walked into the coffee shop for the second time that day in a daze, engulfed by her thoughts of what had just happened and how foolish she had been. She ordered her coffee almost mechanically and went and sat in her usual spot by the window.

Looking out she could see couple after couple walking past in the sun, holding hands and enjoying being with one another, oh how she envied them. In the distance she saw a familiar car, the one she'd vacated only 5 minutes or so before, driving away in the opposite direction. She knew she was worth more than a backseat fumble, but old habits die hard.

Brushing away the lone tear that crept down her face she regained her composure and began sorting through her files trying to get them back into some sort of order. Her love life might be one big mess, but her business sure wouldn't be.

CHAPTER 2

Jane sat in the restaurant waiting for her dreaded appointment. She'd made sure to get there nice and early to try and focus on exactly what she needed for the profile set-up. It was proving to be extremely difficult to stay focussed after her encounter with William.

Her head was all over the place and she really needed to make sure she got this right. Joanna did, after all, have the capability of reducing her and her company to ashes. She worked for the local newspaper as a critic and just loved criticising everything. She didn't even leave it to within work hours, her whole life now seemed to be work.

In a way Jane felt sorry for her. She'd been widowed in her 30's, her late husband lost his life in a tragic car accident on his way to work. They had both been so career minded they hadn't gotten round to having children, so it was just Joanna. Because of that she threw herself into her work and she'd made quite a name for herself along the way.

Jane admired her, just carrying on and making herself so successful, despite everything she had been through. Joanna Wilson's name alone could put the fear into any business owner. She sure as hell didn't want to be featured this week.

There were questions she wanted answering and wondered if she could get away with slipping them in as part of the set up. Things like why she never re-married, or even dated another man since Steve passed. Even her mother thought it strange and had, on several occasions, tried to set her up with any eligible bachelors she could. She even tried Andrew Blake! Despite him being twenty years her junior, there was also the fact that she didn't even know him which meant she was seriously running out of options and was willing to try anything.

Joanna and Julie, Jane's mum, had been friends since they were young and had been through everything together. Jane wondered if her mother knew about their meeting today? She wouldn't be able to find out either, unless she brought it up, client confidentiality and all that.

She looked up just in time to see Joanna's tall slender figure walking past the window. Dressed head to toe in Chanel, she hoped she looked like her when she was in her sixties. The super glamorous Joanna entered the restaurant and instantly the waiters stood to attention. It was as if a member of the Royal family had just walked in.

As she was led her over to their table Jane stood to greet her. They made the usual ritual of 2 air kisses (Joanna would hate it if contact was actually made) and half a hug.

"Jane darling, so very nice to see you. It has been a while since you have dined at your mothers, you know you really should make more time for her, she misses you terribly." Joanna never thought she spent enough time with her mum. Even if she were to spend hours there every day, it still wouldn't be enough. This could be the part of Joanna that gave away her secret unhappiness with the fact that she herself never had children.

"I was just thinking about calling her later today actually. I've have been meaning to go see her for a few days now, but my schedule has been really full, dinner dates with clients - you know how it is."

"And what about dates for you dear?" She asked, casually looking over the wine menu.

"Nothing really to report there. I am meeting someone this evening but he will be the first for a few months. After William and I ended, well lets just say things have been pretty quiet in that department." She wished she hadn't said anything. Why had she mentioned William? Why had she mentioned her date tonight? This was bound to spark an interest with Joanna and the raised eyebrow and eager look meant she was now about to be grilled about it. Just what she needed!

"Yes it was a shame about William, he was such a nice man. Handsome, good income, and you both looked very good together. Tell me again, why did that end?" Jane could tell this wouldn't be the only question she would have to answer on this topic and tried to think of the best way to sidestep it. After all that had happened with him today, the last thing she needed was to talk about him now with what appeared to be his number one fan. She wanted to get back to why they were both really there. Joanna's search for love, not hers.

"We wanted different things." *Yeah, he wanted orgies every day and night and I wanted a steady relationship,* she thought bitterly.

"Really? I thought you two were a perfect match. Well as perfect as you can get these days. They don't make them like they used to. Take my Steven, no-one has ever lived up to him so I just gave up believing that anyone could." She had the look in her eye. The one she always had when she spoke of her late husband. Each one filled with so much sorrow and pain. Jane hated it.

It was in that moment she understood why Joanna had never re-married. Her soul was eternally linked to Steve's and no-one else would ever come close. So why now? She was about to ask but Joanna, sensing the question was coming, quickly added.

"Well that is until now. I feel now is my time dear and I'm not getting any younger am I?"

This was obviously a rhetorical question, if she answered she would only offend her. No, a simple smile in this instance would suffice. Joanna's quick reaction however had piqued Jane's interest. Something wasn't quite right.

The waitress came over to take their drinks order. Obviously intimidated by the mere presence of Joanna. Stammering at first she eventually managed to get her words out.

"Hello ladies I hope you have found the wine list satisfactory. Are you ready to place your drinks order?" It was evident she was nervous, for one thing she couldn't stand still. Shuffling from one foot to the other, but still trying to sound professional. Jane could tell Joanna had noticed too as she began narrowing her eyes in her direction.

"What would you recommend?" Joanna asked abruptly. So, she had opted to test the poor girls knowledge of the wine list, see if she knew what her favourite drink was. Any place that had got so much as a notion of praise, which was so rarely given by her, knew this basic information. She prayed this poor girl had been prepped before waiting on them.

She had made it clear who the booking was for well in advance to make sure they were prepared. She'd half expected them to call and cancel, something a lot of places did once they heard who would be attending. An odd look was creeping over the waitress' face, she was panicking. It looked like she was searching every nook and cranny in her brain to locate the information she was after.

"Well madam, we have a beautiful Romanée Conti and a Montrachet Grand Cru but as we know you are quite partial to a Chateau d'Yquem, which we have ordered in especially for you, should you wish to have some today." Jane exhaled deeply, having not even realised she'd been holding her breath throughout the whole awkward interaction. When Joanna wasn't looking she grinned and gave a congratulatory wink in her direction. They had done their homework after all.

"Very satisfactory, I do like it when a place goes that extra mile. Two glasses and two house salads then please."

"Oh just one please. I never drink during lunch. I like to keep a clear head for my other appointments. Just a sparkling water for me thank you." The last thing she needed was to have her judgement impaired, especially around Joanna, who knows what she might end up agreeing to.

"So, tell me more about this date you mentioned this evening..." Why couldn't she let this drop?

"Oh it's nothing serious, just dinner with someone I met last week. It's not all that interesting. Should we get back to business or wait until we have eaten?" Jane thought she'd successfully steered the conversation back on track, but Joanna was like a woman hungry for information and wasn't going to let it go.

"Oh! Well you never know how things are going to pan out do you dear. So….. have you seen much of William lately?"

Actually I saw him today Joanna and we had sex on the back seat of his car while it was parked in a side street, was what she really wanted to say, knowing it was a sure fire way to shut he up. Sadly, this was still a business meeting.

"I hadn't seen him for a while but actually bumped into him in the coffee shop near my office earlier today. I really need to get things started here as I have other appointments today." She tried to to sound as polite as she could but the constant questions about William kept bringing it all back.

The feel of his hands on her body, the taste of him on her lips, the feel of him sliding deep inside her. Coughing quietly and shaking her head she brought her thoughts back to the restaurant and their meeting. She really needed to stop talking about him.
If she could just stop thinking about him.
He was bad for her she knew this, why couldn't anyone else see it?

The waitress brought over their food and Jane pulled out her IPad ready to begin. She knew she needed to be thorough to be in with even a remote chance of finding a good match for her, but the time was ticking on. Even if she'd wanted to she couldn't sit here all afternoon. Time was money at the end of the day.

"Firstly I need to know a little bit about you, likes and…" She really didn't want to say dislikes, she knew there wasn't enough time to list them *all* during this meeting. Only problem was, she couldn't think of an alternative quickly enough.

"...dislikes, but I already have a lot of your background from knowing you my whole life so you can just email the office with this section. The main thing we need to get out of today is what you are looking for in a prospective date."

"Well I'm not really sure what to say.." She bit her lip as if trying to work out the best way to say whatever it was that was racing through her head.

"I know, why don't you tell me what you would look for, then I can see what sorts of things I might need to tell you? Yes that sounds like it would be best, doesn't it Jane? It has after all been a very long time."

She was shocked, she'd never in all her time doing this job, been asked this question and she hadn't a clue what to say. Taking a bite of her salad to allow herself more time to think it through, until she eventually had no option but to answer.

"Well this all really needs to come from you Joanna. I can't be seen to be giving you ideas, then your match might not be valid, do you understand?" *Phew, got round that one,* she thought happily.

"Well I promise not to tell if you won't!" Smiling in such a way that told her she was going to have to answer.

"I don't exactly have a brilliant track record but, if I was looking for 'The One' then he would be kind, loyal, have a good sense of humour, you know, all the usual things. He would be successful but the job isn't really that important, as long as he has ambition." Jane was lost in a dreamy state. Realising she'd been describing all the usual cliché's, it dawned on her it was probably the reason that she hadn't come across her Mr Right and had only settled for Mr Right Now.

"Well that all sounds delightful, I wouldn't mind any of that." Jane groaned. Joanna had done exactly what she didn't want her to and now wanted. She had put ideas in her head and invalidated the whole damn profile. She hadn't had time to work out the best way to get round any of this when Joanna spoke again.

"Do you know Jane, I think I actually know someone who might be perfect for *you.* He works in my office and has been single for a little while now. Far too young for me of course, but I think he would be just perfect for you." Joanna looked pleased. Taking a few mouthfuls of her drink before slowly raising her fork to her mouth, she added.

"I am sure he would love to meet you and he ticks all your boxes from what you have just described." The satisfied smile on her face as she ate her food explained that the sole purpose of their lunch meeting was for this very reason, and this reason alone. She didn't take her eyes off her but didn't look like she had anything more to add, Just simply waiting for her to respond. She'd been caught off guard for the second time that day and she wasn't sure how to react.

"Joanna that is very kind but I already have a date and don't usually make it a habit of seeing more than one man at a time. It would reflect badly on the business." Satisfied with her answer and glad she had finally found the ability to speak she broke their eye contact and continued to pick at her unappetising lunch. Looking at her watch she wished the next 30 minutes would hurry up so she could get back to the office and speak to Libby.

"I understand that darling but you said yourself that the date this evening wasn't anything serious. How about you say yes to meeting Neil if nothing comes from this one tonight? That way the ball is in your court so to speak."

Hearing her phone ringing, Jane took it as a welcome break from the awkward situation Joanna was trying to force her into.

"I am sorry Joanna it's the office, I really need to take this." Standing abruptly, she moved to the front of the restaurant before answering.

"Oh Libby you are a lifesaver, thank you so much for calling, is everything alright?"

"Yeah everything is fine here, I just wanted to check in and make sure you hadn't killed yourself or Joanna for that matter." Jane could hear the amusement rising in her voice. She wanted to tell Libby everything there and then, just talking to her seemed to have a way of making things seem alright again.

"Well it's safe to say that this whole meeting is a sham. I will see if she actually wants a profile set up or not and will try and get back to fill you in, there isn't going to be enough time right now. In fact…" She glanced through the window and could see that Joanna was getting impatient, tapping her fingers sharply on the table in front of her. She knew she was going to have to go back in.

"I am going to have head back in Hun, she looks like she is about to whip out her laptop and review me right now."

"Quick get back in, that's the last thing we need, not when things are going so well!" It was good to joke about these things but the reality of it was that Joanna could crush her and her company with just one simple article. Hurrying back to their table she smiled as she seated herself opposite once again.

"So sorry about that. So, would you like to re-schedule a profile set up for another time?"

"Darling we both know I only got you here for your love life and not mine. I simply won't take no for an answer on this. Neil really is a catch and you have done a lot worse when left to your own devices."

Not sure how she felt about being spoken to so honestly, she decided to just agree and save an argument. All she wanted now was to get out of there. She could always say that things went well with Ben and she would never have to hear about this Neil bloke again.

"Ok Joanna you win!" She knew the two words 'you win' would make her happy so she started gathering her things together ready to leave.

"If things don't go well with Ben, then I will call you to arrange something, *but* if I like him and we go on further dates then I will have to give it a miss."

"That is perfect my dear, I look forward to hearing from you soon then." Jane decided not to reply, simply motioned to the waitress to get the bill.

"Jane dear, this wasn't really your meeting so lunch is on me, you will be thanking me once you have met Neil." Grateful she didn't have to fund Joanna's expensive taste in wine on this particular occasion, she decided to let the second mention of Neil slide.

Making her excuses, she said her goodbyes and left. Praying she wouldn't have to hear from Joanna for a long time. She stepped out into the street and headed back to the office. It had been a bad start to the day and her mood was beginning to reflect it.

CHAPTER 3

"Hi Jane, you're back earlier than I thought. I expected the dragon lady to hold you captive. So was it really as bad as you thought it was going to be?" Jane could tell Libby had been watching the door ready to pounce for all the juicy details. She had such a wild character, always the first to get any gossip on anyone but also the first person to be there for you in a crisis. She was, what you would call, petite, with wild curly red hair that aptly matched her fiery personality, but she was also loyal and Jane really couldn't ask for more in a best friend. She was more like the sister she'd never had.

"Worse actually, somehow she managed to turn the meeting into a match making session for me. I think I managed to brush it off as I already have a date tonight with Ben, and thankfully my rule of not seeing more than one man at a time really came in handy." Realising she had yet again mentioned her date tonight to someone that would want to know everything, she hastily added.

"…But I had to say that if I wasn't going on any further dates with him then I would go on one she set up with this Neil guy from her office." Thinking that Libby would want more information on the deal with Joanna she waited impatiently for her response. Libby just looked confused, seemingly trying to recall some piece of information. Jane wasn't sure what it could be.

"Hold on a minute. Firstly who is Ben and since when did you have a date? Were you even going to tell me, or just sneak out? Secondly, how dare Joanna waste your time!" Folding her arms she turned her head away to glare out of the window.

"Lib calm down. I met Ben last weekend in The Swan and to be honest, the moment I left I haven't given him a second thought. He called me after I left the office earlier, just before I went to the coffee shop and bumped into William, else yes I would have called so you could help me pick out an outfit!" Knowing that Jane needing wardrobe help would satisfy Libby who loved nothing more than putting together the perfect outfit.

Libby had always wanted to be a clothes designer and had got a first class honours degree in fashion at university. Sadly, the closest she'd gotten to working with clothes was her sales assistant job in Zara, which she only took to have a regular income. Life was expensive in London and although her parents were well off, once she'd graduated her parents told her she had to stand on her own two feet and grow up. They'd always hated her choice of study and Jane thought they wanted to prove what an awful choice she had made studying fashion rather than accountancy like her father and brother. So, making her live off her own means would show that she had wasted three years of her life on something that couldn't support her. Then when she begged them for help they could cart her back to Uni to study a 'proper' degree.

"You could have text!" *At least she's smiling,* Jane thought, *she can't be that annoyed with me!*

"Erm, especially as you bumped into William!! That should have been a definite text, its been like what three or four months since you guys ended hasn't it?" *Crap*, Jane thought.

"It was nothing, just bumped into him as I was going in to the coffee shop, he was on his way out."

"Did he notice you? Of course he noticed you, what a silly question. What did he say? Are you seeing him again?" Libby was over excited and wouldn't rest until she had *all* the information. Jane felt exhausted, today had been the strangest day she'd had for ages and she just really wanted it to be over already.

There was a gentle knock on the door and, grateful for the interruption, Jane went to answer in person. Opening the door to see Jamie on the other side.

Jamie always looked uncomfortable lately. He was so tall and slim that he looked gangly and out of place everywhere he went but recently things had gotten a lot worse. He seemed to have withdrawn, like they were strangers, not two people who had known each other for years. She felt sorry for him, he was an introvert with zero self confidence but balanced Libby perfectly, which explained why they made such a perfect match.

"Jamie, hi how are you? Haven't seen you around the flat lately, hope I haven't scared you off by being home so much?" Jane realised that having not dated for months she'd been spending an awful lot of time moping around at home. The more time she spent there it seemed the more time Libby and Jamie spent at his place. Not that she minded, she hated being the third wheel.

"Hi, ah no just want some quality time with Lib that's all." He wasn't making eye contact. He'd always been a bit odd, but he made Libby happy so she turned a blind eye to it for her sake.

"You ready for lunch babe?" He nodded towards Libby who was just tidying some paperwork. She looked hesitant, like her need for gossip was greater than her need for food. The stern look from Jane made her decide that food was probably the best option.

"Sure thing Pookie, let me just file these and I will be right with you. I'm feeling some Nando's goodness, how 'bout you?" Libby had just been paid so she always celebrated this with a slap up meal at her favourite chicken restaurant. In a couple of weeks she would be lucky to have any money left so would be settling for an apple, or whatever Jane got for her.

Slamming the filing cabinet shut with a satisfied bang, Libby grabbed her purse, gave Jane a brief peck on the cheek and flung her arms around a shocked and embarrassed Jamie. He was never one for public displays of affection.

"Come on Pookie, mamma wants some chicken." With that they headed out the door. Leaving Jane, thankful she hadn't had to talk about her moment of weakness.

***

Libby and Jamie entered the tube station and hand in hand they jumped on the escalator taking them down to their platform. After being together for ten years they were comfortable in each others silence and didn't need the idle chit chat that usually accompanies any new relationship. It had been a good five minutes since they left the office and neither had really said much to each other. Libby could handle a few minutes but anything over five was pushing it.

"So how has your day been so far? Jane has hardly been in all morning, the life of success hey.." The change in Jamie's composure was instant. Something had gotten his back up and Libby wanted to know why.

"Yeah work has been good, almost finished developing this game for a new client which will please William no end as he can finally get the big cheque from them." He said William's name with disgust. It was no secret that he disliked his boss, setting up such a huge company at a young age and earning so much when knowing absolutely nothing about actual gaming made him sick. He reckoned that he had probably never even played one in his entire life so wondered why he'd wanted to set up a business in that area in the first place.

It was something he would never know, it wasn't as if they were buddies and he could just ask. Jamie had worked hard to get to where he was but was still barely making ends meet. Being the minion he got paid a minimal amount of the huge money paid to the firm each month, William obviously got the biggest cut. He knew how to schmooze the customers to land the big contracts but would be totally screwed if he lost Jamie and Daniel who worked, along with temps, to develop the ideas and get the products made, tested and ready for sale. Jamie was even starting to work more with the marketing guys to get the packaging up to scratch as he knew each game inside out, something which he never got any recognition for. If he didn't love his job and have the belief that one day he would catch a break, then he would probably have given it all up a long time ago. He also didn't like change so that was another reason he'd stuck with it for so long.

"Well that's good, does that mean you will be going out of town to present it to them?"

"More than likely, but it should only be for a few days." Libby immersed herself in work talk the rest of the way to Nando's.

Finally when they were tucked away in their corner table she broke into her usual bout of gossiping.

"Speaking of your boss, Jane saw him today. First time in months since, well since, you know…. She was just in the middle of spilling the beans when you came to take me to lunch. Have you seen him this morning? Has he said anything?" Libby's excitement was surfacing when she realised she might be able to hear the story after all and not have to wait to hear it from Jane.

"Yeah he mentioned he had, erm, bumped into her this morning." His tone gave him away. Something had happened and he knew about it.

"Jamie is everything alright? What has happened?" She had never seen him like this before, he was normally so laid back and nothing much really affected him.

"Well if you must know, my boss and yours have reached an all new low in my opinion." He couldn't even bring himself to say William's name.

"What has Jane got to do with William? Did something happen? Oh my god what happened?" Libby twigged what Jamie wasn't saying and wanted the whole story. Well from William's side anyway, she would have to get Jane's version later.

"Well lets just say that an old flame was rekindled but if I were to repeat the exact words he used it would put us both off our lunch."

"So, wait a minute, are they back on? But she has a date with Ben later? What do you mean? It's like you are speaking in riddles!" Libby had all sorts of scenarios racing through her mind. If she didn't get the story soon she was likely to explode. Sensing it Jamie put her out of her misery.

"Well to put it bluntly, boy meets girl in coffee shop, boy propositions girl, girl goes running to a quick back seat shag which boy then tells our whole office about before going off to one of his usual lunch dates that we then have to endure hearing about as well. Just cause we are graphic designers does not mean we need the graphic fucking details! Seriously he must be one of the biggest jerks I have ever had the misfortune to be associated with and why Jane has no self control around him I do. Not. Know…. She knows what he is like! I mean his car…… in broad fucking daylight?"

Libby hadn't been expecting this, she was thinking maybe a bit of a kiss and a fumble at the most but full blown sex! In a car! In the middle of the day! This didn't sound like her. William on the other hand, she knew was no stranger to a bit of risk taking, he'd even tried it on with her once. Asking her to go to the toilet and wait for him so they could 'play'. This had been while he was with Jane too and she was that shocked she didn't tell anyone. She'd had to avoid the toilet for the whole night in case he followed her in, she didn't want to give him the wrong idea.

Jane had been cut up when she discovered what he was like and swore to never let a man use her again, yet here she was one wink of an eye and she was right back in that very same place. Libby was pissed with her and wondered if Jane would've really told her the full story or some PG rated version?

"What?? I can't believe it, after everything he did to her she just jumps right back into bed with him? No, I won't believe it till I hear it from her. You know what William is like, always embellishing things to make him look like a stud, but I just can't see it, not after everything, surely she wouldn't?" She hadn't meant it to come out as a question she just found it so hard to believe. She thought Jane was better than that.

"Well the way he was talking made it sound pretty real, apparently she was, now how did he say it? Putty in his hands." He'd always hated Jane's string of one night stands, they were the main reason he stopped going over to their place. If Libby was earning a bit more he would suggest that they move in together, but she was so dependent on Jane's income and with him barely earning enough to feed himself let alone Libby too, meant this wasn't an option for them just yet.

"That's vile, if she did go there again how does that make her look to him, how desperate would she have to be to do it? I really don't get it!"

They ate their lunch in silence both angry for different reasons. Jamie, angry that his boss felt the need to tell them every minute detail, and Libby angry that;
1) Jane could do something like that and,
2) that she hadn't trusted her enough to tell her.

She was hoping that Jane hadn't left for her next appointment by the time she got back else she would have to wait until she got back from her date and that could be any time, if she came back at all. Sitting and wondering, did she in-fact know her at all anymore?

***

Libby rushed back to the office knowing that she would be leaving any minute to meet Dean. Jumping off the train without even saying goodbye to Jamie, running up the escalator as fast as her little legs could take her.

"Shit!" Reaching the barrier she realised she hadn't gotten her Oyster Card. Rummaging through her purse she felt the panic rise when she couldn't find it. What if Jamie still had it? It felt like ages had passed and she knew it would be close if she was going to catch Jane now.

Her fingers finally located it right at the bottom of her oversized bag which she was now regretting choosing for that morning. Clutching it as tightly as she could so as not to drop it she scanned it over the detector and pushed her way through the barrier. Ignoring the yells of,

"Hey where's the fire love?" that followed. Her run turned into a sprint, she knew her time was running out.

When she broke free of the underground she raced down the street to get back to the office. Along the way she began to wonder why it was so important to hear it from Jane. There wasn't much that Libby ran for so why was this so important? Her lungs burned as she tried to satisfy them with oxygen which she was struggling to inhale. She needed to speak to her, that was the bottom line of it all.

Pushing through the door and taking the stairs two at a time she finally reached the door.

"Damn it."

Locked.

She'd left already.

Grabbing her phone she opened up a blank message and punched in;

*How could you Jane! We **NEED** to talk!*

As she pressed send she hoped Jane would get it before her meeting started.

CHAPTER 4

Jane was sitting in the coffee shop waiting for Dean, she always liked to be early for her appointments. The thought of an already lonely person sitting by themselves waiting for her made her feel quite sad. She also knew that some of her clients would be extremely self conscious about sitting alone so she wanted to make sure they were all as comfortable as she could possibly make them. One of the things her clients loved about her were these personal touches. Chasing love is a hard enough race at the best of times, but it's even harder when you have to employ someone to help you reach the finish line.

Taking a sip of her skinny caramel latte she savoured the full flavour, the richness of the strong coffee combined with the sweetness of the smooth caramel, it was sheer bliss. It's captivating aroma intoxicating her as she brought it to her lips almost making her forget the events of the day. Enjoying the warmth of her favourite drink as it slid down her throat, it quite literally warmed her from the inside out. Feeling it spread through her gave her a momentary happy glow. A glow she only got from two things. Coffee and sex.... She couldn't be sure which she preferred the most.

Most people got their glow from alcohol but she wasn't really much of a drinker and couldn't remember the last time she'd actually gotten blind drunk. She hated the feeling of being out of control. And of course there was the fact that hangovers get worse the older you get. So being on the brink of turning 30 the thought of having a hangover made her feel as rough as the hangover itself would.

The more coffee or sex she had, the more she wanted. They were her personal drugs and she'd been abstaining from one until this morning. Trying not to think about her moment of weakness, thinking she had cleared her head back at the office, but thinking about sex just brought it all back. Her cheeks flushed and she felt flustered all over again.

Seeing her phone flash on the table pushed all thoughts of naughty liaisons to the back of her mind. It was just a text from Libby, but It was a welcome distraction from her wandering thoughts. Checking Dean wasn't walking over she opened it only to be shocked with what she saw.

Libby was angry with her? *Why?* Racking her brain she tried to think what she could be angry about. She checked the message again in case it hadn't been meant for her.

No, her name was clearly there. But she hadn't done anything that could have upset her, she hadn't even seen her since before she went on her lunch with Jamie…… Realisation dawning that the news upsetting Libby could have come from Jamie.

She'd totally forgotten that Jamie worked with William. But he wouldn't have said anything about what happened to him would he? *What kind of man goes bragging about shagging an ex he hasn't seen for months?* No that couldn't be it, William was a lot of things but he wasn't the sort of person that would divulge information unless it was necessary, especially to a work colleague. She hoped this was the case as she was forced to push it all to the back of her mind as she saw Dean approaching.

"Dean, how lovely to see you again. I ordered you a cappuccino, that's what you drink isn't it?"

"Yes perfect thanks." Dean looked agitated and she hoped it was the meeting and nothing more making him feel this way. Remembering she hadn't actually heard from his date Louise either, meant that she was going into this meeting blind. The whole situation was starting to make her feel anxious.

"So we only have thirty minutes and the purpose of this meeting is to just catch up with you and see how things are going and to find out how your date with Louise went last week, she seemed really great for you, don't you think?"

"Yes Libby filled me in about today. To tell you the truth Jane, it didn't go well. I am sorry to say that we just didn't seem to have anything in common… We want different things out of life and I genuinely cannot see how you could've thought we were a good match……… we were just so… so different."

She felt like she had been smacked in the face. She'd not had a negative comment like this for five years. Not since the business had really found its feet. She had always been used to satisfied, happy customers. To hear that these two people were polar opposites and yet she'd sent them out on a date together meant something had gone seriously wrong.

Had she pulled the right file? Had Libby called the right Louise to set the date up? It had to be an error, She couldn't see how she could have made such a huge mistake. Rifling through her briefcase she pulled out both Dean and Louise's files, grabbed at the paperwork inside and quickly started reading through it, ignoring the fact that Dean was sitting there waiting for a response.

Crap! It was there in black and white, they were completely wrong for one another. Looking up she saw Dean waiting expectantly, all the colour draining from her face as she wondered how she was going to get round this.

LIE!

Lie Jane until you get back to the office.

"Dean I am so sorry but I think there has been some sort of filing error. Erm, was this the lady you met with the other evening?" Showing him the photograph on Louise's file. Dean glanced at it and without hesitation nodded in agreement.

"Ah, ok so no filing error then. I will have to check with Libby to make sure the correct Louise was phoned. We keep a call log back in the office and we have a couple of other Louise's on our books at the moment so I am thinking it's maybe that. I know that doesn't solve the issue we have here but at least if we know what caused the problem, we can fix it."

She felt flustered. Wanting nothing more than to speak to Libby ASAP but quickly recalling the text message she'd just received from her. She knew if she were to call her now she would be on the phone for an eternity trying to get to the bottom of her angry tirade. No, she would have to check it all herself.

"I will check it personally when I get back to the office. I am so so sorry Dean I honestly wouldn't knowingly have set you up with this woman. There has to be some underlying issue here I just can't see what that is right now. We will offer you another set up free of charge if you are willing to take that as some form of compensation?"

"I don't know Jane. Last week was pretty hard going. After….well you know…" He'd confided in her that he hadn't had a relationship since his wife passed away a few years ago. It had knocked him so much that he found it hard enough just speaking to women. He'd tried other dating agencies before, both online and face to face before deciding that Love Games was his best option, and now she had just let him down. It wasn't any wonder he wasn't biting her hand off for the offer.

"Dean I assure you I will find someone and I won't set anything up until I am 100% sure that everything is as it should be this time. Please Dean, this has never happened before, you only have to read our reviews over the last five years to know that. This is a complete one off." Even she could hear how desperate she sounded.

All she knew was that one bad review now would destroy everything she'd worked so hard to build up over the past six years. Ok so the first year there had been a lot of ups and downs, teething problems at best and she had almost given up on it all. But she worked hard and now, five years on she hadn't gotten a single bad review.

"I'm really not sure. I was so embarrassed by the whole situation. I don't think Louise was too pleased either. This isn't a game despite what the name implies, these are peoples lives you're dealing with!" He wasn't being very co-operative, but then why should he? He had paid good money for something and he wasn't satisfied with it. Jane was appalled that what he was saying was true. She felt sick to her stomach.

"Dean I won't get this wrong again. Trust me….please?"

After what seemed like an eternity, he looked up from his cappuccino. The one he'd been staring into for the majority of their conversation, not wanting to make eye contact with her.

"Ok, last chance Jane. I can't go through this again. I just can't."

She made further assurances to Dean. She wouldn't let him down this time. Finishing her latte she was glad the meeting had ended and she could get out of there.

The weather had changed drastically from earlier that day when it was bright sunshine. The sky was now full of clouds and it was starting to rain. Thinking that today would have been a good day to call in sick as she made her way back to the office through the crowds of people barging past her trying to dodge the shower that was growing heavier with each step she took.

***

"Certainly, whatever you need for your event we guarantee to get it within budget… absolutely. Can I pass you back over to my assistant Rebecca to set up the meeting? …Well it sounds like Signature Events are the people for you. I look forward to meeting with you in person so we can go through all our ideas…. Goodbye." Putting them on hold, he used the intercom to let Rebecca know what was needed before transferring the call over. He could have let one of his employees deal with the call but the truth was he liked being hands on.

He'd taken over Signature Events when it was about to go out of business in order to help the elite plan high-end events with the huge budgets that go with them, not to just sit in his office telling others what to do. His clients liked the fact that the owner of such a renowned company got his hands 'dirty' and actually did the work he advertised. It also helped that a lot of his clients were female and his dashing looks and impeccable manners meant he was always the one chosen to plan their events.

Over the years it made him hugely successful and extremely wealthy along with it. He took a look around his enormous office. Minimalism was his thing. In the vast space he had to work in he simply had his desk, chair, and a few bookcases which housed all his favourite literature, not that he had much time for leisurely reading these days, but he felt comfortable around books. They were some of his prized possessions.

Rebecca, his assistant, had a small desk in the area outside his office and it was her alone who single-handedly planned his life. She kept the employees in check and made sure things were done to target and budgets were adhered to.

If it hadn't been for Rebecca he would still have been married to Carol. He shuddered at the thought of his ex-wife. It'd been her who informed him of the illicit affair his wife was having with one of his younger employees and then helped him to set up the plot to catch her in the act.

That was almost eight years ago now and he hadn't been able to trust a woman ever since. Sure he had been on many dates but due to his wealth and notoriety the women he ended up attracting just wanted the lavish gifts and lifestyle, rather than the man that gave them. He wasn't asking for much was he? He just wanted someone to love who loved him back. Total, all consuming, unconditional love, just like in the literature he so coveted.

Noticing the light flash off on the intercom he buzzed back to Rebecca.

"Rebecca can you come in here for a moment please?"

"Of course Mr Blake, right with you." She answered almost immediately, always the professional even after all these years.

She hadn't been with the company for very long when the whole Carol drama happened. Fresh out of university and so very eager to learn, he took her under his wing and they'd developed the best work relationship he'd ever had with an employee.

But that was all it was. Yes, she was attractive. Sleek brown hair that glistened when the sun caught it, and a figure most women would kill for; but he had never seen her as anything more than a trusted and much valued employee.

There were rumours of course, especially when people realised it had been Rebecca that spilled the beans about the affair. Everyone thought she was using it as her chance to step into Carol's shoes. But after a while, seeing that nothing was going on, the gossip eventually died down and normal service was resumed.

He could still remember the day that she'd knocked on his door asking for a private word. She had looked so uncomfortable and it was the first time she hadn't made direct eye contact with him. He could recall word for word that timid speech she'd obviously been practicing all morning.

"I'm not sure the best way to say this Mr Blake."

"Jut say it as it is Rebecca you know I like straight talking people."

"It's.....a difficult topic for me to bring to you that's all."

"I'm all ears."

"I am sorry to be the one to have to tell you this. But....well....it's just...."

"Rebecca I don't really have time for this, either spit it out or get out."

"I have seen Carol with Peter from accounts."

"She is often in the office, but I don't see what the big deal is about her talking to my employees Rebecca!"

"No you don't understand she was *WITH* him, you know they were....canoodling."

Canoodling. A word he wasn't familiar with but now believed was probably the nicest word the poor girl could think of for what she'd witnessed.

At first he hadn't believed it. But, with the help of Rebecca who'd worked out a pattern to the meetings, he was able to witness it for himself. He was devastated, utterly heartbroken and for the first time since starting AB Incorporated, he took time off. He had gone away, left his phone behind and had no contact with anyone from the office, or even his family for that matter. He'd needed to get his head together, work out what to do.

When he got back Carol managed to persuade him to try marriage counselling. Needless to say it didn't work and they ended their marriage shortly after. As a result of that he was guarded around women.

The only one he trusted was Rebecca. She was the one person who he could speak freely with and who would speak freely and honestly back. She had no ulterior motive, she wasn't after anything more than her career so could be trusted 100%. It had been her idea to go to Love Games as he needed a respectable date for his next big event and also because she knew that above all, he was lonely.

There was a knock on the door and she strode into the room. His eyes as usual were drawn to her body. He was only human after all and she was so easy on the eye. He knew every man in the building would have given their right arm for a night with her, but she was so naive she just took all the flirting as friendliness.

"Mr Blake, what can I do for you?"

"I have a meeting with Jane Aldrin from Love Games this afternoon and would like to go through a few things with you. I shouldn't let her know who I really am unless I'm sure I can trust her." He thought back to some of the women he'd encountered over the past few years.

During the first couple of years after his marriage ended he had been off women altogether. After a bit of coercion from his peers he eventually made the decision to get back out there. He took out various women he met in high class wine bars. Taking them to places like The Ivy, showering them with gifts and spending nights in luxurious hotels, but he soon grew tired of that lifestyle and admitted he was really searching for someone to settle down with. The only problem was that he now had a reputation for being a ladies man and because of this, only attracted a certain type.
The gold digger.

"Of course, where would you like to start?" Pulling her notebook and pen out of thin air, she was poised and ready.

"Right so first name won't give anything away, there are lots of Andrews! How about Andrew Smith? No amount of googling with that name will be able to lead anyone back to me. It won't be until they meet me that they might make the link. By that point I will have hopefully had at least one successful date."

"Sounds good, so Andrew Smith it is. So, what do you do for a living Mr Smith?" She was jotting down notes as he spoke, making sure to capture the whole conversation. He was dreading this meeting but at least he would be fully prepared thanks to her.

"Management, I doubt at this stage she'll need anything further do you?"

"It might be an idea to think of something just in case." She had a point and he deliberated while Rebecca waited patiently.

"Ok so I manage a group of people in…. insurance." That could be passable, he had previous experience in insurance so he knew enough to make it plausible. She nodded in polite agreement.

"Marital status will surely come up, how do you want to handle that one?"

"Divorced, many people are these days so at least that's one thing I won't have to fake." He hated the term 'divorced', it made him feel like a failure and he hated to fail. It was a constant reminder that he couldn't even keep the woman he loved happy enough to stay with him. He would have to try to not let this bitterness show when he met with Jane. He didn't want her thinking he was a total loser.

"Do you think that will be enough to get going with?" Rebecca sensing he wasn't willing to go any further started to close her notebook and get ready to leave.

"I think you will be fine, just remember this is just a meeting for you to find out about her and her company, you only have to divulge what you want and *then* you can make the decision if you want her to work for you or not. Just because you are meeting her doesn't mean you are tied into anything." Her fondness for him was evident. You could tell by the way she looked at him. There was always a sparkle in her eyes when he was around and she had thrown her all into her work just for him.

"Thank you Rebecca, that will be all. Can you let me know when I need to leave? I am going to be busy here for a while, I will undoubtedly lose track of the time."

"Of course."

She smiled and left the room, Andrew watched her peachy bottom sway from side to side almost hypnotising him as she walked away.

The phone ringing on his desk snapped him out of his trance. It had been a while since he had been with anyone sexually, he wasn't usually *this* bad around a good looking woman. Feeling his nether regions twitch in admiration of the sight his eyes beheld, he cleared his throat and picked up his phone.

CHAPTER 5

Jane braced herself as she pushed open the door to the office, ready to take the bullets that were about to fly the moment she stepped inside, although still unsure why they were firing at her in the first place. She didn't have long before she would have to leave again, but she wanted to know what was wrong and hopefully try and sort it out. Libby's fiery personality meant that when she was pissed off she was awful to be around, especially if it was you she was pissed off with.

Taking a deep breath she forced herself to enter into the firing line. Libby had obviously been watching the door, she hadn't even waited for her to come into view when she heard the screech.

"JANE HOW COULD YOU?? I am so angry with you I could throttle you! Please tell me it's all bullshit, please say it's not true!" She was red in the face, almost as red as her hair, which was saying something as she always chose the brightest shade when she went to her colourist. She'd been stewing on this for some time, now it was bursting out of her like a volcano erupting, set to cause utter devastation along the way.

"I have no idea what you are going on about and I don't have much time before my next meeting. Do you want to just cut the crap and tell me what this is all about?"

"One word Jane….William! Second word Jane…..car, ring any bells?" So William had shot his mouth off then, *bastard.*

The events of the day were starting to take their toll and everything felt like it was moving in slow motion. She was angry as hell, mainly with William but also with Libby, she just wanted to scream back at her. *What's it got to do with you anyway?* It was no secret that Jane'd had a lot of one night stands, but Libby never reacted like this before. *Why now?*

"I was about to tell you earlier but Jamie arrived. How was I supposed to know he was going to broadcast it to the whole fucking world?"

"So it's true? I thought you had more self respect than that."

"Yes, I had a moment of weakness, but it's not a crime. I needed to have sex and that's exactly what I did. Nothing more nothing less. I don't see why it's such a big deal? It was just an urge that needed satisfying like when your hungry you eat, when you're horny you have sex. Seriously *what* is the problem?" Jane was shouting and was sure people on the street below could hear her through the open window.

"Jane this isn't you, can't you see that? You were so cut up about him after last time. You want love, I know you do, but you won't find it by jumping into bed with every single person you meet." Her words were coming out through gritted teeth. So, the truth was out, Libby thought she was an easy lay. Her one true friend who she'd always been able to rely on, thought she was a slag.

"I don't get why this is all being said now? After the amount of one nighters I've had before, what is so different about this one?"

"Because it was with the one man that hurt you so much! The one man that made you realise this wasn't the life you wanted! Plus there is the fact that it was in broad daylight on the back seat of a car for God's sake. If that doesn't spell cheap I don't know what does. I mean did you even speak to him or just open your legs to make way for him to slide in?"

SLAP

Her hand made contact with Libby's cheek, she felt the tingle from the force she'd put behind it. She had never hit anyone before and hadn't expected it to hurt her as well as the other person.

"You're just jealous because your love life has become stale after ten years and you wish you had some spontaneity in it!"

Libby stood, her hand caressing her cheek, unable to speak.

Jane wished she hadn't said it, as soon as the words came out, she knew she didn't mean them. It was true, she wanted what Libby and Jamie had, it was what she'd been searching for but just couldn't find anyone she felt she could commit to. She hadn't come across anyone that made her go weak at the knees.

"I'm so sorry I didn't mean it. I understand what you are saying, I just had a moment of weakness. I didn't mean to hit you I…"

"We'll talk later, you need to go."

It wasn't often that Libby didn't want to talk so Jane knew not to push her now. She did however need to leave, or she would be late.

Picking up the folder Libby had prepared, she reached over to give her a hug, but pulled back instantly as she turned away from her.

She hated leaving things this way, but on this occasion she had no choice.

~

Sitting in the wine bar waiting for her next client, her head pounding furiously, she rubbed her temples, thinking just how fed up she was with getting to an appointment feeling like she was all over the place. Using the time to look through the folder she remembered she didn't know anything about this man. Libby hadn't gotten anything from him on the phone apart from his first name so this folder wasn't much use after all.

She sat for five minutes or so with probably her hundredth coffee of the day, just staring around the room. Feeling a tad silly she reached into her bag and took out her iPad.

The sound of a gentle cough made her jump. Looking up she saw the most beautiful man she'd ever seen in her entire life. Yes he was much older than her but she couldn't stop as her eyes slowly took in the perfectly styled hair, bright blue eyes, masculine jawline, the clearly well toned body hiding underneath his exceptional suit and for a moment, she was rendered speechless. She wondered why this man was standing by her table? Had it been reserved for him and she'd accidentally sat there?

"Excuse me, are you Jane..Jane Aldrin?" Feeling her insides flutter as the silky voice spoke her name.

"..Ye..Yes that's me." It quickly dawned on her that this must be Andrew.

"You're Andrew?" The disappointment was evident in her tone. Surely this man didn't need help finding a date? Taking a look around the room she noticed there wasn't a single woman in the bar who wasn't captivated by him. Remembering her manners she quickly stood to shake his hand, this was, after all, a business meeting.

"Yes the one and only. I apologise for my tardiness, I had a telephone call that kept me longer than I would've hoped." He sat down not taking his eyes off her and an embarrassed Jane followed suit. She couldn't stop fidgeting, this meeting was going to be tough. Every time she looked at him she was completely lost for words. *Stick to business and you will be ok,* she kept telling herself.

"Ok, so you are here to learn more about Love Games and what I can offer you. First I will need a few details from you to gauge how best I can help…"

There was no reply, just a nod. He was being quite awkward. He wouldn't look her directly in the eyes and kept glancing around the room like he was worried someone would see him there with her. It threw her train of thought so she quickly went back to her notes.

"We have your Christian name but no surname, so how about starting with that?"

***

"SMITH…Andrew Smith!" He spat back at her, pleased he'd remembered his cover name in time. He'd almost told her his real name. He hadn't expected to be blown away by the woman he was meeting. All he could think when their eyes had met was, i*s she single?* His eyes dropped to her hands as discreetly as he could manage….. Nope, no rings to be seen. Still, she might be in a relationship. He had to find out…. but how?

He couldn't concentrate on anything she was saying to him, he just wanted to know more about her. This urgency to know if she was single, what her favourite food was, her favourite books, films, he needed to know absolutely everything. The feeling was alien to him and he didn't like it.

It took him a few moments to realise she'd asked him a question.

"I'm sorry, could you repeat that, I didn't quite catch what you said?" Now he felt like a total arse. He'd taken his eye off the ball, he could have slipped up about his true identity. This was too risky, he was going to have to keep this short and sweet and get the hell out of there. First Rebecca getting him excited and now this total stranger? What was happening to him?

"No problem, I just need to find out a bit about you so we can work out the package that would best suit what you are after. If you are looking for the basics then the minimal package would be best, but if you want a one to one set up then we have a full works package which would suit you. We have several other packages as well, it all depends what you are looking for. Have you had any thoughts so far?"
You!
I want you all over me.
I want to feel those pink lips locked onto mine.
I want to feel your hands rubbing up and down my back pulling me deep into you.

He realised he couldn't look at her. Each time he so much as glanced in her direction these wild thoughts took over. The urgency to get this over and done with had been heightened.

"Full." Unable to manage more than a one word reply, he waited for the next question.

"Right, that won't be a problem. The full package offers you an extensive profile set up with me which then gets paired to other profiles that best suit what both parties are looking for. We will make contact and set up your first date and have regular catch up sessions to discuss any questions you might have before and also after the date to discuss how it went or if you want anything changing on your profile etc."

Only half listening now he wondered how he was supposed to sit through more meetings with this woman when he couldn't even look at her? The thought of never seeing her again helped make up his mind.

"Perfect."

***

Jane was confused. Initially he'd come across as super confident, but after their initial earth shattering eye contact he hadn't looked directly at her since. To say she was intrigued by him was an understatement. His one word answers gave her the impression he was hiding something.

"So would you like to tell me a bit about yourself so I can start getting to know you Mr Smith? It's always best to have a little bit of information before the profile set up." This was only partly true, she wanted to be in the best position to help find him someone, of course, but her compulsion to know more about him was stronger than her professionalism on this occasion. He was definitely hiding something, she just needed to figure out what.

"I think it best we leave it at that."

"It really would make things run smoother if I knew more about you. Your age? Where you work? Are you divorced? Widowed even? Things like that, nothing too deep, just the basics, then I can leave you with the paperwork and it will be up to you to decide if you think Love Games is for you." She knew there was a slim chance he'd be signing up but she stayed hopeful. At least if he didn't she would know she'd tried her best.

"40, divorced, management. Will that be all?" With his last words their eyes locked once more.

She felt all the breath leave her lungs. They were truly the most beautiful eyes she'd ever seen. Such a dazzling shade of blue that even the oceans in Hawaii would be jealous. They were like two pools of perfection she just wanted to dive into. Fully aware she was staring she quickly broke their connection and casted her eyes down to her murky drink, everything seemed duller after staring into them.

She could feel the heat burning in her cheeks as the blush she wished she had control over, crept across them. Not wanting him to see she bowed her head lower. Afraid to look up again in case she was entranced once more, she managed to mumble a few words she prayed he would be able to hear.

"That should be enough yes. Thank you for your time, I look forward to hearing from you whichever way you decide to go."

"Of course. Thank you. Goodbye." With that he stood up and stalked out of the bar leaving a mesmerised Jane behind him.

It took several minutes for her heart rate to go back to some resemblance of a normal pace. Gathering her belongings and thoughts, she got up to leave. Musing on the meeting, she felt satisfied she couldn't have done any more with him. If, by some miracle, he signed up, then she knew the profile set up would be tough. It would be like trying to get blood out of a stone trying to get him to open up.

She thought back to the information she had managed to prize from him.
He was divorced.
What stupid woman would leave that? She honestly couldn't see a single flaw in him. He was gorgeous, well dressed and that voice! Three perfectly good reasons NOT to get divorced.

Walking past a news-stand she glanced up. She never read newspapers but something was pulling her eyes upwards.

There he was. There was that beautiful face staring back at her from the front page of one of the daily papers. Stunned she stepped forward eager to read the headline,
My night with Andrew Blake.

Scanning the page she saw a much smaller image of an attractive young woman. She was young, incredibly slim and oh of course she was blonde. Just his type. It then suddenly dawned on her. The name. Andrew Blake!
The Andrew Blake!

There was no denying that the man she'd just met was him. He was Andrew Blake, renowned business man and owner of the highly successful AB Incorporated. *So that's what he was hiding but why does he need me and why the fake name?*

Pretty sure the way he'd acted meant he hadn't been the slightest bit interested once he met her, and not divulging anything about himself, was a clear indicator that she wasn't going to be hearing from him again.

Grudgingly she pushed him from her thoughts, at the same time reaching in her purse for money to pay for the paper which she then proceeded to stuff to the bottom of her bag. Further down the road, she suddenly stopped to wonder why she had just felt the compulsion to buy it? Why did she care about some blonde bimbo shagging that wonderful man? *Yeah that wonderful man who lies to complete strangers that are just trying to do their jobs!*

Thank God the day was over. This had been one of the shittiest ends to her working week. Too many pointless meetings and one almighty row with Libby meant she was ready to curl up in bed and eat just enough chocolate to make the crappy feelings subside.
There was a beep from her phone.

One new message.

Knowing it wouldn't be from Libby, they still had a lot to say to each other before she would text, she opened it to see who it was from.
Can't wait for tonight. Ben xx
Ugh, Ben! Why do I keep forgetting about Ben?

It wasn't long before she was back at the office and ready to lock up for the weekend. Once inside she was glad to see that Libby had already given up and gone home, thankful that round two of the slanging match could be postponed. Slumping down onto her chair she put her head back and closed her eyes. She could feel the tension building at the bridge of her nose. She knew the events of the day had caused it and truthfully, the last thing she needed now was a date.

She sat considering what her chances of hiding away in the office for the entire weekend were when she noticed the answer machine light flashing.

Clicking the button to see who it was, she melted as she heard the familiar, dreamy voice, of Andrew Blake echoing out of the tiny speaker.

"Jane, I want you."

The message didn't register. She kept playing it over and over. All she could gather from his brief message was that he wanted to sign up after all. *How unexpected.*

She'd come to the conclusion she would get either a call from his office on Monday or an email outlining the many reasons he would have for not going any further with his application. Jotting a note in her diary to call him next week, she locked her desk, glad to finally be heading home.

CHAPTER 6

Libby was fuming, storming into the flat, she'd found it really hard to concentrate after what'd happened with Jane. All she wanted was the cheap bottle of wine she'd hidden in the fridge and to be bale to immerse herself in some drawing. She was only truly happy when she had a blank canvas in front of her and the peace and quiet she needed to be creative. Something she didn't get much of living here.

Not that she wasn't thankful, Jane had always been there to look after her and she knew she wouldn't be able to afford anything in London without help from either her or her parents, which she wasn't going to ask for any time soon. She wished she could break free and go it alone, stand on her own two feet for a change and be fully independent rather than just pretending to be.

In all her 28 years she hadn't accomplished a great deal and her dreams of becoming a designer were so far off they seemed so unbelievably unachievable. The only thing she had succeeded in was her relationship with Jamie. Then remembering Jane's harsh words and feeling slightly nauseated at the fact that she'd actually sat and thought about them over and over again. She couldn't argue the fact that they weren't true, not when she *herself* believed them. The realisation had hit her in full force.

She was bored.

She did wish for some excitement and spontaneity, but after ten years was that even possible?

You always hear of old married couples in their single beds rather than a double. She wasn't even living with Jamie and already felt they were at that stage of their relationship. She couldn't even remember the last time they'd had sex. Was Jane right, was she really only upset with the whole William thing because she was jealous? She really hoped not, the day she wished to be used for someones personal pleasure would be the day they checked her into a mental health clinic as something would be seriously wrong with her.

Smiling as a funny image of herself in a straight jacket flashed into her head, she wondered what she should do that evening. Not wanting to leave the flat until she'd sorted things with Jane, but not sure if she would even venture back before her date left her in a quandary.

The sound of 'Moves Like Jagger' rang loudly from inside her bag. She reached inside for her phone.

"Hiya Jamie" Answering her phone automatically knowing it would be him. *See no spontaneity* she thought.

"Hi Babe, you been home long?"

"No, not really. I'm just about to get into my sweats and will probably order pizza seeing as it's pay week and all that." She suddenly remembered the way she'd left him on the underground.

"Oh, sorry about earlier too, I had to speak to Jane and turns out it's all true, we had this huge argument and haven't spoken since. I'm waiting to see if she comes home before her date later so we can talk some more."

"She has a date and she's still going after what she did? I feel sorry for that poor bastard." He had come to believe that a date with Jane ended up with a good bedroom work out.

"Hey! She doesn't always put out on the first date, she isn't as bad as you make out. I know I always moan about her and the way she is, but she is just lonely." She'd shocked herself by defending her after everything that had been said, that and the fact that her cheek was still sore from the slap. But the truth was she cared too much about her friend and no-one, not even Jamie, was allowed to say anything remotely negative about her.

"Well her choice in men leaves something to be desired, I mean William? Jeez it was bad enough the first time round seeing them all over each other everywhere we went, I can't go through all that again, no chance."

She thought back to the last time Jane had been with him. She'd fallen for him big time. He was good looking, had a reasonable sense of humour and by the sounds of it, knew how to please a woman in that oh so special way. Libby could see why there was an attraction and although she would never admit it to anyone she had been slightly jealous.

Living with Jane in a two bedroomed flat that had paper thin walls meant her multiple orgasms could be heard quite clearly through them. On most occasions it had been while she was lying, cramped up, next to Jamie who was snoring his head off, blissfully unaware of the heat and passion happening next door.

Jane had been infatuated with him and although she would've never used the words herself, Libby was sure that she'd fallen for him.

When she found out about all the other women she'd been completely devastated.

Having never seen Jane so down before, Libby hadn't known how to help her. She was turning down dates with men that could've lifted her back up and she barely went out unless she was pushed into it. It had only been during the past couple of weeks that she'd started being herself again and actually venturing out socially.

"Well she knows a bit more about him this time round doesn't she. I don't think she'll be falling for any of his tricks." Defending Jane was having a calming effect on her and she could feel her anger subsiding. At this rate when she got home Libby would be back to normal with her. Well apart from the slap maybe, that would take some serious grovelling to forgive.

"Yeah well we'll see won't we? So what time are you coming round, it's been ages since we had some….. ahh…. alone time?" She could hear his goofy smile through his voice, knowing full well what he meant by it. *Great* Libby thought, *the one time that's on the cards and I am going to turn him down.*

"Actually babe… I have some work to do tonight so I was going to stay here. I hope you don't mind? There are a few things I need to sort out and with Jane going out I thought I could use the opportunity to get them done." She didn't go into too much detail, she knew he wouldn't question her or want to know exactly what she was working on at home when he knew full well that Jane insisted all work was to be left in the office, especially at a weekend.

"Oh, right well I guess I will make other plans then. Don't work too hard babes, see you tomorrow?" Libby, ever thankful that he was so trusting. Not that she would normally keep things from him, there were just some things she didn't feel ready to tell him yet.

Stepping back into her room she pulled her art folder out from underneath her bed. It was the only place in the flat that she knew Jane would never look. They'd shared this flat together since leaving University. *A quaint yet delightful two bedroomed flat* was how it'd been advertised in the property details and in the excitement of renting their first, non-uni related, property in London, it made them overlook the fact that the place was no bigger than a shoe box.

The living room and kitchen were open plan to give the illusion of space but once their furniture had been moved in, they realised they were going to have to be quite economical with the space they had to work with.

Starting off with the bare essentials they gradually built the place up to how they wanted it. Thankfully they both had the same tastes in interior design and loved everything vintage shabby chic, so all their furniture was either white or cream and distressed.

Libby had opted for the smaller of the two bedrooms, given that Jane was pretty much paying for it and she was chipping in as and when she could afford to.

One of the many reasons Jamie preferred her to go round his was the fact that she only had enough room for a single bed. In the early days they'd thought it quite fun to squeeze into her microscopic room and have a fumble on the floor as they didn't want to risk falling off the bed, before cuddling up under a quilt that was barely big enough to cover the both of them. It was a good job she was so tiny, if she'd been the same size as Jane there was no way they would've been able to both fit.

Jane's room wasn't much bigger, but at least she could fit a double bed in, along with a wardrobe and the smallest dressing table the world has ever produced, leaving just enough room to manoeuvre around it all to make it a liveable space. Jane's room had the en-suite too which sounded glamorous, but was simply a toilet and wash basin and only just enough room for a tiny bin.

Despite the size issues it was their home and held many a happy memory, which is why neither had even so much as thought about moving anywhere bigger. Her room was her safe place, the place she could shut the door on the reality that was her life and dream about making it big in the fashion industry. Something she planned to do that evening.

Hearing the door click open she quickly stuffed the folder back under her bed and walked back to the living room to face Jane. She desperately wanted to make up with her now but first she had a few things that needed to be said.

CHAPTER 7

Jane was relieved to be home, the feeling of closing the door on a shitty day almost made her date later on seem bearable. Turning around she saw Libby emerging from her bedroom and instantly felt awkward, as if she'd walked in on something she shouldn't have. Regretting how things had been left earlier she wasn't sure if Libby would even want to talk to her. Rooted to the spot she realised she was going to have to make the first move, she couldn't just stand in front of the door all evening.

"Hey……you ok?" She took a tentative step towards her, dropping her briefcase and handbag on their perfectly upholstered sofa before Libby responded.

"Look, I don't agree with what you did, in fact I think you were pretty damn stupid. I just know you are worth a million of him and he really doesn't deserve to have someone like you at his beck and call."

She'd been expecting more shouting, crying even, she had after all been a super bitch earlier. Her kindness and understanding threw her.

"I am so sorry, what happened earlier, I didn't mean any of it I was just so angry. I have had THE worst day ever today and the last thing I needed was the third degree for something which I know I fucked up with. When I saw him I intended on ignoring him but that man just knows how to work me! After then going back and telling his whole fucking office means the only action he will see from me again will be my replica Chanel boots as they connect with his balls."

She couldn't help giggling at she thought of the satisfaction she'd feel doing it to him but knew, deep down, she would never dare to go through with it. Libby was smiling too. They'd obviously both conjured the same mental image, William in one of his poncy suits trying it on with her again and her retaliating with a swift kick to his genitals. It was a definite ice breaker and it seemed to do the trick at clearing the frosty air between them.

"Jane, you know you would never do that but how funny would it be!!" Libby couldn't hold back any longer and her laughter burst out. She had a comical laugh. It was so funny that anyone around her had no choice but to laugh along too. Unable to stop, she joined her, throwing her arms around her shoulders, thankful they were back to normal.

"So, I know I am angry and all that, but I need to know. How was it?" *Ahh,* Jane thought, *Libby's hunger for gossip has resurfaced and she wants all the gory details.*

"Well, what can I say, it has been a while since I....well you know! All I can say is that *she,*" She motioned towards her crotch, "was more than ready to be played with. It was almost embarrassing actually, it was like she took on a mind of her own." So much had happened since then that it almost seemed like a dream now as she recounted her moment of raw passion..

"And, was he as good as you remembered?? Come on don't hold back on the details Jane, the amount of times I heard it all first hand anyway I might as well have been in the room with you guys!"

A coy smile crept onto Jane's lips as she recalled a personal joke her and William had shared that one day they should invite Lib in to join them rather than have her spend the evening alone having to endure listening to them at it all night. At least for her it had been a joke, but she was now fairly sure that William had actually been serious. She wouldn't put anything past him after today.

"Erm, well it was good yeah, but like I said it really was more satisfying an urge than anything else. We started off kissing, hands wandered, as they do, then one thing led to another and I just sort of jumped on top of him." She blushed at her admission and turned her head away to hide her embarrassment.

"But it was what it was and that's it, nothing more, nothing less ok, now can we please stop talking about it and forget it ever happened? I need to shower and get ready to meet Ben."

Libby was annoyed but knew she wouldn't get anything more out of her now.

"Sure hun. So what's this Ben like? Are you excited? I can't believe you forgot you even met him, that's quite funny actually, the poor bloke has probably been plucking up the courage to call you and you forgot he even existed."

"Well...I don't really know much about him. I'll be able to fill you in later if you are still up, if not then in the morning for sure." She smiled knowing Libby would try and wait up for her but would fail as she always did and wind up fast asleep on the sofa. She would then pounce for information the moment she woke. She was always the same when Jane went on a date, but as it had been so long since she'd been involved in the whole dating scene she knew Libby would be a million times worse for this one.

"Ok, go! Go shower and I will start looking through your wardrobe." Libby shouted at Jane's back as she disappeared into the bathroom. Quickly calling for her pizza before disappearing into Jane's room.

Turning the shower on to warm up, Jane peeled off her clothes. She wanted nothing more than to wash away the events of the day and a long shower usually did the trick. Jumping in and pulling the curtain closed around her, she stepped under the hot steamy water. Feeling all her muscles relax as water gently cascaded over them. Bit by bit the tension that had built up melted away.

Using the time to reflect on her weird day she realised that this one had been a record breaker for bad business and bad decisions. Hoping it was a one off she thought back to William and felt disgusted with herself, forcing herself to push the images to the back of her mind she told herself that it never happened. The more she thought it the more she would believe it was true.

Her thoughts then wandered to Andrew. She suddenly remembered the newspaper stuffed in her handbag and wished she had time to read it. Telling herself the first opportunity she had she'd read it. If she was going to be working for him, so to speak, she wanted to know everything about him. Well that and the fact that she sort of had a crush on him. But why had he given her a false name, what exactly did he have to hide?

Thinking about him brought back the excitement she'd felt the moment she first saw him. He was beautiful, a real life silver fox and she just couldn't get him out of her head. She felt her cheeks flush. Thinking back to the way he looked in his suit, his slightly greying hair only making him more alluring. Jane wouldn't usually look at an older man like that, so not her type, but it appeared that when it came to him, she couldn't help herself.

The more she thought about him she found herself becoming aroused, losing herself in the feelings as she imagined his piercing blue eyes and the way her insides melted when they locked on to her. In that moment he had her captivated.

Unable to stop she lost herself in her imagination. Seeing herself drawing closer to those wondrous eyes until their lips were touching, recalling his scent, allowing it to intoxicate her senses to the point she became dizzy. She needed him.

Before she knew what she was doing she began touching herself. Carefully massaging her breasts while she imagined what his lips would feel like around her nipples, the thought alone making them tighten in pleasure. She gently tweaked one making her nether regions tingle with anticipation, excitement and longing.

Moving her hand down so she could circle her clit, working herself until her legs began to shake and her breathing became shallow. Although she was in the shower she could feel how wet she was getting.

Conjuring up a picture of what she thought his body would look like, knowing it would be exceptional from the way his suit had clung to it, in that moment she longed to feel it pressed tightly against hers. Embracing one another under the hot water. His manly hands all over her with an intense look in his eyes, telling her the next step was full penetration.

She was close to reaching her climax. Curious as to how big he would be and how he would feel sliding inside her, almost took her over the edge. Unable to take anymore she thrust a finger inside herself imagining it was him, hard and throbbing in anticipation for his own release. With just two masterful strokes she was sent over the edge, thinking about her orgasm rippling over him as he filled her made her cry out in sheer ecstasy.

Shuddering as her orgasm reached its end she opened her eyes, bemused by what had just happened. This man was a total stranger and she'd never fantasised about anyone before, let alone had one of the best orgasms of her life over them.

"Jane?? Jane are you staying in there the whole frigging night?? Jeez come on else you will be late and I want my compulsory fashion show before you head out girl." She was brought back to her senses by Libby's shouts. Hoping she hadn't heard her cries of pleasure she quickly washed and jumped.

Wrapping a towel around her and putting a second in the standard turban style around her dripping hair, she ambled into the living room in a daze to find Libby scoffing away at her pizza. *Had that meant anything? Do I really fancy the hell out of one of my clients? A client that's lied to me about who he really is?* There was one thing she knew for sure, this was going to end badly.

CHAPTER 8

She decided on one of the many outfits Libby had put together for her. Opting for the only one that made her look like she wasn't trying too hard to impress, but still showed she'd made some effort. She went for a pin striped pencil skirt and red peplum top combination along with a classic Chanel style cardigan and matching clutch.

Jane loved designer clothes, but having never been able to afford to buy the real thing, replicas were the next best thing. Always on the look out for the most authentic looking ones to add to her ever growing collection, the Chanel cardigan had been her latest acquisition.

One day she hoped to be able to walk in and buy the real deal. Telling herself that everything she'd read about the law of attraction were in-fact true. The more you wanted something and actively believed you were going to have it, then the universe would give it to you. She'd been actively thinking in this way for many years now and was still stuck with her replicas. Thinking about it she wondered if she should be focussing her positive thoughts on finding a man. Then again clothes and accessories were less likely to hurt her so they seemed like the better horse to back.

Taking one last look in her full length mirror that had beed carefully concealed behind her bedroom door she applied her signature red lipstick, grabbed her clutch and sauntered into the living room. She knew she looked hot and that made her confidence soar.

"Twit twoo, how hot do you look??" Libby jeered at her as soon as she was in view.

"Girl, your fashion designer should get a medal cause you look totally amazing….oh wait that would be me." Smiling at her and shaking her head at her usual outburst.

"Ok, ok enough! Do I really look alright? I'm so nervous, you know not really knowing much about him after everything that went on before." She had started to get butterfly feelings earlier but hadn't been sure if it was nerves or just the smell of Libby's pizza making her stomach growl. Now she had no doubt about it. She was nervous.

"You look amazing, you know you do, now go! Go and have a great time. You deserve it after today ok. Let your hair down and get mamma some gossip!"

The more she thought about it she realised she did need this, she hadn't dated for months and felt she'd almost forgotten how to. This was her chance to get back in the race and start chasing the love she truly wanted.

She eventually found the restaurant just off Leicester Square, but realised she didn't know what name the table had been booked for or even what Ben's surname was for that matter. She decided the best option would be to loiter in the entrance and wait for him. Her insides fluttered as she watched couple after couple brushing past her to start their dates, *oh what it would feel like to be in love,* she thought bitterly.

She was suddenly overcome with a sinking feeling, the thought she might be stood up. She was sure they had agreed 8pm. It was now almost 8.15, she wondered how much longer she should give it before giving it up as a bad job?

Shit, but what if I got the time wrong? Or am I stupidly at the wrong restaurant?

Quickly opening her clutch to find her phone when she felt a hand gently brush the small of her back. Feeling her entire body tense she looked up. As soon as she saw his face it all came back to her from the night they'd met.

Thankfully, he was good looking but he certainly didn't have the same effect that Andrew had on her. Disappointed she made an effort not to write him off, just because he didn't make her insides melt didn't mean it wouldn't happen. *Rome wasn't built in a day Jane!* She mused.

"Ben, hi. I was just about to call you, make sure I had the right place. This place doesn't have a bar and I wasn't sure what name the table was under else I would've gone in…" Realising she was rambling she stopped herself before she looked like a fool.

"Sorry I'm late I was finishing up a shoot."

"Oh, are you a photographer?" Jane knew how stupid the question was as soon as it escaped her lips, just looking at him told her as much. He was too good looking to be behind the camera.

"Ha ha, no I am a model. I mainly work abroad, in Paris actually, but my agent managed to get a cheeky shoot in while I'm back."

He was kinda cute when he laughed, had little dimples on his fake tanned face and, oh wow, what white teeth he had. *All the better to eat you with my* dear flashed into her head and she stifled a giggle. No, she really didn't fancy him. Models just weren't her thing, she liked normal guys and he was no ordinary guy.

"Erm, shall we go in I'm starving?" He motioned towards the door and waited for her to go through it. *Hmm, clearly they don't teach models about being a gentleman these days*, Jane thought as she pushed through the doors and waited for him to follow behind her.

Finally getting seated at their table they ordered drinks. She'd decided to take Libby's advice and let her hair down so agreed to getting a bottle of wine between them. She wasn't a big drinker and sharing a bottle meant she would have to have a few glasses so would be rather merry after them. It was the weekend and she'd had a shitty day so why not?

The conversation wasn't flowing but he was nice to be around even if he wasn't saying all that much. Believe it or not the silences weren't uncomfortable and for two people who had only met once before, they were quite relaxed with one another. *Surely you are supposed to have some excitement, some chemistry if you fancy someone?* She thought. *You shouldn't be this comfortable on a first date!* It was all wrong and deep down she knew it.

He was looking at her expectantly. Realising he must have asked her a question while she'd been lost in her thoughts.

"Sorry, it's quite loud in here. Did you say something?"

"Yeah I asked what you were having?....You know, to eat."

"Oh, I haven't even looked at the menu." *Whoops*, she'd been staring at the menu for a good 5 minutes but didn't have a clue what was on it. Looking across the table she noticed he hadn't even picked his up. Was he not going to eat? What, just sit there and watch her while she devoured hers? She hoped he wasn't one of *those* models.

"Erm, are you not eating?" Motioning to the unopened menu in front of him.

"Of course, I just eat here quite a lot so I already know what I am having." It was the first time Jane had been to Sartoria's and she took this opportunity to have a good look around.

It was a swanky place, not somewhere you would just pop into if you were hungry and happened to be walking past. Mainly because you couldn't really be just walking past, it was tucked away off a little side street, so unless you knew it was there, you weren't likely to stumble upon it by chance. Still, it was extremely busy with happy couples and groups of friends starting their weekends. There was copious amounts of alcohol flowing on each table and the varying scents of everyones meals drifted in the air making her stomach lurch as she contemplated what to have herself.

There was a piano in one corner, tucked away under a huge potted plant that threatened to take over the entire restaurant if left to it's own devices. It was only then that she realised the beautiful music she could just about hear over all the chatter was actually coming from that piano. She'd been forced into taking piano lessons as a child but had been awful at it, she was virtually tone deaf but still appreciated classical music and the feelings it could evoke.

The lighting dimmed and a lilac hue shone around the room. It was just bright enough that you could see what you were eating, but dim enough to make it feel like you were the only people there.

"So what are you going for? There is so much to choose from, what's recommended?" Scanning the menu there really was a lot of choice. Hats off to the poor chef who certainly had their work cut out. It had everything from Italian foods to Thai and even Indian and Mexican. Libby would hate it, far too much choice. She would be there for a good hour or more before narrowing it down to probably three or four dishes, then another hour before she actually ordered anything, only to regret her choice when it arrived at the table.

Thinking about Libby she realised that she was at home, alone, and the fact that she was eating pizza meant she wasn't going out and Jamie wasn't coming over. Not sure why she was staying home on a Friday night alone she realised she'd emptied her glass of wine, unaware she'd even been drinking it in the first place. She was going to have to slow down, a novice drinker indulging on an empty stomach would be disastrous.

"The house salad is amazing here so that's usually what I go for."

Salad???
A house salad???

She blinked a few times and bit her bottom lip. She was trying her hardest not to burst out laughing, now she knew he was in-fact a stereotypical model, wearing a tight white t-shirt to set off his spray tan and also help set off his dazzling white teeth. His brown hair was expertly coiffed and probably had more product in than her own. That was saying something as she had pulled hers back into a french twist which required a *lot* of hairspray to keep those rebellious hairs in order. He was well built too and clearly looked after himself, going to the gym and eating nothing more than a bloody house salad. *Has he never heard of a treat night?*

Maybe it was the wine or the fact that she'd had such a bad day, but she found the whole situation extremely funny and, struggling to fight back the urge to burst into a fit of laughter, she downed another half a glass of wine. Now feeling the effects of the one and half glasses of wine already consumed she knew she would need some serious stodge to help soak some of it up. She also secretly wanted to see what Ben's reaction would be when she ordered.

"Shall we call the waiter over?" She smirked, wanting to make sure that she wasn't the only one to witness his reaction. She couldn't work out why she was finding it so funny, but she was finally starting to relax and have a good time so she didn't really care.

He didn't make any attempt to move, just nodded and sat looking at her expectantly. Once again she was going to have to do the work. Motioning to the nearest waiter that they were ready to order with a polite smile, the young boy headed towards their table.

"Sir, Madam, I take it you are ready to order? What can we get for you?" Jane hadn't expected such a well mannered response from someone that was blatantly still in college.

"House salad, no dressing please and hold off the bread roll." She'd opened her mouth to give her order but Ben had spoken first. How does someone that must have had a lot of dates NOT know that the woman orders first? Jeez this guy could do with one of the dating masterclasses she offered some of her less experienced clients.

"And for the lady?" The waiter turned to face her and raised an eyebrow. She was glad he was here to see this, at least it would give him something else to talk about other than her dates atrocious social skills.

"I think I will go for the pasta special please and I *will* take my bread roll with that. Actually, you may as well bring me his too, don't want to see it go to waste." Unable to control herself as she saw Ben's eyes widen across the table, she placed a hand to her mouth and pretended to cough while she stifled the giggles that were about to break free. Of course she would never eat both rolls but seeing his reaction was just too good an opportunity to miss.

"Oh and I think we will probably be needing another bottle of this too." Motioning to the almost empty bottle she was holding before pouring out yet another glass for herself. Wine would certainly be needed to help her get through this. Looking around at the pudding tray, she knew it was something she didn't want to miss out on even if she would probably be the only one on her table having any.

The rest of the dinner went better than anticipated, she found that he was surprisingly easy to talk to. He didn't say much but did, at least, appear to be listening intently to what she had to say. She hated to admit it but they were comfortable with one another which only meant one thing, they were destined to stay in the friend zone. Not that she minded.

With the conversation, and wine, flowing freely it wasn't long before she was drunk and, not wanting the evening to end, managed to convince Ben to go on to some bars.

Jane couldn't recall any time she'd ever enjoyed being drunk, she normally felt so out of control and the spinning rooms made her feel she was suffering with vertigo, not a carefree individual having the time of her life. Tonight however she was loving every minute of it. That feeling of being able to conquer anything gave her the courage to even attempt some flirting. Ok so she knew she didn't fancy Ben, but why not use him for some practice?

Feeling elated and uninhibited she danced to her favourite song and grabbed Ben to join her. She didn't care who was around them, just enjoyed living in the moment, every second devoted to that short moment of happiness where nothing but the rhythm and beat matters. She felt his body close against hers as she executed some of her best dance moves and became overwhelmed with an urge to kiss him. Holding herself back she pondered why it was that she was unable to control her sexual urge today?

Lost in the music, her thoughts wandered to the amazing fantasy she'd had in the shower. Before long she was wet and tingling for some attention. Wrapping her arms around Ben she threw her mouth on his. The loud cheer that erupted around her made her kiss him harder. She tried to prize his lips apart so she could slip her tongue in but felt nothing in return. His mouth stayed firmly shut.

Ben gently pushed himself backwards and out of her grasp. Looked into her eyes, shook his head and began to walk back to their table.

"What the fuck?" She muttered to his back as she marched after him, darting her eyes around to make sure no-one had noticed her embarrassing rejection. As soon as he reached the table Ben picked his glass up and knocked it back in one swift movement. An enraged Jane barged up to him as best she could in her drunken state, quickly regretting the 6 inch heels she'd decided to wear.

"What the actual fuck Ben?" She was slurring and tried to sound as sober as she could but it was proving very difficult. She'd lost count of the number of drinks they'd had, but he seemed stone cold sober as he stood facing her now.

"Jane, it's not that I don't fancy you, man I would give nothing more than to take you into that corner…." Nodding to a dark corner where they would be concealed from everyone else.

"BUT, you are way too drunk it would seem like I was taking advantage! That's just not my style."

"Oh so now you find your chivalrous side!" Jane spat back at him. He looked confused but she didn't stick around to hear what he had to say next. Marching up to the bar, which thankfully was quite empty given that most people were still rocking away on the dance floor, she ordered as much as she could to make her forget what just happened. She drank shot after shot as they were lined up on the bar and continued to do so until she did just that…. forgot.

The happy glow had faded, she was now drinking with a purpose. Humiliation did not sit well with her and she needed to make it disappear.

CHAPTER 9

Opening her eyes slowly, she winced as light filtered through them. It was like having an electric current flowing straight from the window directly into her brain, so intense she could cry. Peeling her tongue from the roof of her mouth she wanted to fill the bath up with ice cold water and drink the whole lot through a straw. She didn't dare think about what her breath would be like considering it felt as if something had died and rotted in her mouth overnight.

Willing her body to move so she could get out of bed and get some paracetamol to try and help numb the pain, she felt movement next to her. She quickly looked around to make sure she was in her room and hadn't climbed in with Libby next door. Nope, her room, her bed, so who the hell was in there with her?

Praying it was Libby who, after seeing what a state she was in when she got home, had helped her into bed and decided to stay in-case she needed anything during the night. Her mouth was too dry to speak and her body felt as heavy as an elephant's but she managed to roll onto her back and get a glimpse at the person lying next to her.

She didn't remember leaving the club let alone getting home, but was sure she would have some recollection if she'd invited someone back with her? Leaning over she looked again at the enigma lying next to her, it was definitely not Libby.

She could only make out a thick mane of hair on the pillow, the rest of her mystery guest was buried deep in the duvet. *Aaagghhh she screamed in her head, who the hell are you????*

Sneaking a peak under the covers she saw she was only in her underwear and so was the man beside her. So, now she knew it was a man....Had they done anything, she wondered?

"Oh God, oh God, oh God.." She muttered under her breath. She was feeling annoyed with herself. It was one thing to go out and get blind drunk, but it's a whole different story when you wake up next to a guy you couldn't even identify. Jane must have groaned a bit too loudly for the heap under duvet began to move and the mysterious figure gradually became visible.

Jane was left confused. The last memory she could recall from the night had been her altercation with Ben. The very thing that had sent her into self destruct mode and resulted in getting so blind drunk. So, why was he now in her flat and virtually naked in her bed?

Maybe he had a change of heart? Maybe I kidnapped him? I was horny, but seriously to kidnap someone for sex! Surely not.

She was thinking so much she hadn't noticed that Ben had woken and rolled over, he was now facing her. He was staring at her.

"Morning, how's the head?" He was grinning. Flashing those perfectly white teeth right in her face. Never before had she wanted to hit someone as much as she did right then. He was teasing her. Waiting for her to beg him to fill her in on what they'd gotten up to last night.

"Er, it's not too bad actually." She lied, not wanting to give him the satisfaction of knowing she was suffering. Her voice cracked as she tried to get enough saliva in her mouth to stop her tongue sticking again.

"Ben, what are you doing here? The last thing I remember was me being angry and shouting at you?"

"That was one of the last things you did yeah. I didn't want to leave so kept a close eye on you to make sure you were safe and when you couldn't get a taxi on your own, well to be fair you could barely walk on your own, so I made sure you got home safely. You then couldn't get in the door so I helped you up and got you to bed."

"What, and you thought you would just stay over? Did…did anything, you know…..happen between us?" She was annoyed that he'd helped her so much after she was awful to him, it meant she owed him, but it didn't explain why he'd stayed the night.

"Well you were in a pretty bad way and your flatmate was crashed out on the sofa. I didn't want to leave you on your own but didn't want to wake your friend either, so figured I would just stay. And……no, nothing happened. I still stand by what I said in the club, I would never want anyone to feel I'd taken advantage so it's easier to just not go there."

Jane was relieved but still felt a bit weird about him being in his pants in her bed.

"Oh, ahh, thank you for looking after me. It really wasn't necessary."

"No problem. Look Jane, I think we both know we are not going to be dating again but despite everything I do like your company. Could we maybe stay friends and hang out when I'm in the country?"

Ahh that age old line most girls dreaded hearing but at that moment Jane couldn't be happier with those five little words, *can we just be friends?* There was no denying that they'd gotten on and she did feel comfortable around to him. Maybe having a new friend like him would be a good thing.

She used the time to try to get him to fill in some of the many blanks from last night, she feared she she might have mentioned Andrew at some point. Sadly Ben wasn't going to spill any of it this morning.

"It's all forgotten, I had a fair amount to drink as well. Although, you are a pretty good kisser." He winked at her as she tried to turn away to hide her blush. *Of all the things to remind me of it had to be the kiss!*

Trying to be as quiet as they could, knowing Libby would still be sound asleep on the sofa, they crept to the front door so he could escape unnoticed. The last thing she needed was for Libby to think she'd had yet another one nighter. Thinking they'd gotten away with it, she turned around once the door was securely closed only to find her sitting bolt upright on the sofa wearing the biggest grin and a definite glint in her eye. They'd been rumbled.

"Well well well, look what the cat dragged in. And I see the cat brought home a play toy." *Well she isn't mad,* Jane thought happily, that was one thing. She felt rougher than she'd ever felt in her life but knew that delaying spilling the beans would just make things worse. Flopping down on the sofa and snuggling under her blanket she prepared herself for the onslaught of questions.

"I want to know everything, and I *mean* everything!!!!" Libby was too much in a morning, full of beans and raring to go, but today she was like Libby on speed. Jane the polar opposite, was definitely not a morning person. She didn't function until at least her third or fourth coffee and because of this tried to distance herself from Libby until at least this point of the day. Even travelling to work separately was a necessary precaution so as not to start the day off with pointless bickering. So having to face her with the mother of all hangovers, and zero coffee, was going to be a challenge.

"Well where shall I start?" It hurt Jane to think, and Libby's volume wasn't doing anything to help her recall any events she might be able to remember from last night.

"Erm at the beginning of course, duh!"

"Ok, ok just try and keep calm and speak quietly please, my brain feels like its going to explode." Libby put her finger to her lips to signal that she would be quiet as she began recounting the events of the date.

"Well I met him at Sartoria's, which was an amazing place by the way, I can't believe we have never been there before. But he had like zero manners and turns out he was a 'typical model'…He ordered a house salad because that's all he ever has there apparently."

"No way!!!"

"He even held off on the bread roll! So I thought I would entertain myself by having the most carb loaded dish on the menu, pasta, I even asked for his spare roll so it didn't go to waste."

Libby tried hard to stay calm but found the whole scenario so funny she screeched loudly and Jane almost had to leave the room because of it. A warning look made her calm down but she must have been imagining Ben's expression, as she burst into a fit of laughter again and proceeded to fall off the sofa dragging the blanket down on top of her.

"Hey, hungover here need warm, cozy blanket…get off it and get your butt back up here or else I won't tell you anymore."

"Sorry ha ha I just thought of the look on his face……..I'm composed. Wait, gimme some blanket too! Ok, go on…"

"Well despite all that, we did get on well and with the amount of Dutch courage I'd consumed I went in for a cheeky kiss in the club after the meal." She quickly hid her face behind a cushion.

Libby was doing her best to contain her excitement but was fidgeting around so much. You could tell she was trying her hardest not to scream out loud again for fear Jane would stop. She decided to leave her wanting more at this point and let her think the date had gone exceedingly well. It seemed a good place to pause.

"Libby I need coffee." Dragging herself off the sofa she trudged into their little kitchen and flicked the kettle on. She'd always wished they had a coffee machine but there was literally no space for one anywhere so they'd had to settle for instant until they were able to get out to the coffee shop.

"That's ok, I think I can gather what happened next and it's those details I want to hear about Missy!"

Jane smiled to herself knowing how shocked Libby was about to be. Throwing some crumpets into the toaster, she searched the fridge for butter as she waited for them to pop back up all crispy and toasted. Those three minutes felt like an eternity, thinking that if she didn't get some sustenance into her she might actually vomit.

Stuffing half a crumpet into her mouth, she snatched up the other before picking up her coffee and venturing back towards the sofa.

"So????" Libby was literally bouncing up and down in her seat. Those three minutes had obviously been tough for her too. The bouncing made it hard for her to get seated whilst holding her coffee but she managed eventually and continued with her tale.

"Was he a good kisser? How was he in there??" She nodded towards Jane's room.

"Well, he didn't exactly kiss me back."

"What? But then how……? Huh?"

"He kind of rejected me. Said I was too drunk and he wasn't going to go there. BUT he stuck around to keep an eye on me thanks to the state I had gotten myself into."

"But how come he was in your bedroom?"

"He helped me home. He didn't want to wake you but was worried about me so stayed…you know, just in case I needed anything."

"Oh My God! Jane, anything could've happened to you. I am so glad you are alright. Thank God he had the sense to keep an eye on you. He could've just left you there you know!"

"Way to state the obvious there Lib." She laughed. The sensation hurt her head so she soon stopped.

"So he is a model in Paris hey. Might be good for a cheeky weekend away Jane, you know catch up with your new friend in his home town." She let Libby carry on chatting away about how much fun they could have seeing all the sights as she laid back and closed her eyes. It was all getting a bit too much and she tried to shut it all out.
RING, RING, RING…..RING, RING, RING…..

Jumping up with a start as the phone rang, she realised she'd fallen asleep and Libby was no-where to be seen so she forced herself off the sofa to answer it.

"Hello?" She croaked. Still having not had much to drink yet her throat was as dry as it had been when she first woke up that morning.

"Oh Jane, I wasn't expecting you to be there. Is Libby about?"

"Ah, yeah sure hang on." Holding the mouthpiece so as not to deafen him, she shouted for Libby, not knowing if she was even still home. It was Saturday, surely she should be with Jamie? What was going on with those two? She was about to put the handset back to her ear to start questioning him when she saw Libby's door opening.

***

"Coming!" Libby came pelting out of her room and headed straight her her, mouthing 'who is it?' as she took the receiver from her.

"Jamie! Expecting someone else?"

Ignoring her, Libby put the phone to her ear. She seemed almost relieved it was him.

"Hey baby you ok?"

"Yeah not too bad, missed you last night though."

"Oh yeah, what did you get up to? Hope you didn't have too much fun without me?"

"No not much, just went for a few drinks with some of the boys and had a reasonably early night considering it was Friday. I'm hoping you aren't going to bail on me tonight though." He always wanted to spend his weekends with her, but after this amount of time together she relished any time she could have on her own. Sometimes being in a committed relationship was stifling and she rarely had time to enjoy her own company.

Knowing she was expecting an important call later that day and Jane being in an awful state, she would just vegetate in her room or on the sofa for the majority of it, she thought she would be better off staying at home to take it. She didn't want Jane to pick it up and really didn't want to have to answer any questions from Jamie about it.

"Actually babe, I still have some work to be getting on with here so I was going to rain check tonight. Can we meet for dinner tomorrow though? We're going to Mum and Dad's for their legendary roast, you're welcome to tag along if you want? Jane's coming as well."

"What?? She seriously can't expect you to work all week and then keep you that busy that you have to bring work home to do all weekend while she goes out and gets shit faced!"

"How do you know she got trashed?"

"We were in the same club but she didn't see me. I was surprised she was back home after leaving with that guy. She is taking liberties and I think something needs to be said."

He was practically shouting down the phone and she was glad Jane had gone to her room so she wasn't able to hear all the commotion.

"Jamie, calm down it's a one off ok, don't overreact."

"DON'T OVERREACT!! I can't believe you just said that. So I'm overreacting when all I wanted to do was spend some time with my girlfriend and can't cause she is being made to work too fucking hard by her so-called friend?" *Ok so you're in one of these moods are you?* Libby thought. There would be no reasoning with him now he had exploded like this. He was usually a quiet guy, until he was pissed off. Then you would want to steer clear of him at all costs.

"Look, I'm not going to talk to you when you are like this. I will phone you later and if I finish what I am doing then I will come over, but if you are still in this mood then don't hold your breath."

With that she hung up the phone. She'd always been so accommodating for him and even when she hadn't wanted to had always gone out of her way to go see him and given up on countless girly nights to just sit in and eat pizza while he played on video games.

Was she starting to resent him? Sure she had told a few white lies over the past couple of days, but if she had told him the truth, he would want to know all the ins and outs of her plans and why she was doing something about them now. She didn't feel she should have to explain the chasing of her dreams to anyone and hopefully, one day soon, she would just spring it on them all and could bypass all the questioning in the interim.

He did love her, there wasn't anyone that could question that, but he wasn't one for change and a big decision like this would certainly leave him feeling more uncomfortable than usual, making him question everything to the point that she would be so beaten down she would just give up on it. He'd done it so many times she'd stopped talking to him about a lot of things and either got on with them on her own or simply didn't bother at all. This was too big for her not bother with and she'd been given an opportunity to really make a go of it.

Every time her phone made the slightest noise she rushed to it, only to turn her nose up when she found it was yet another text from Jamie trying to provoke a further outburst or a weak apology. She was really waiting for a reply from someone else.

Thinking about it, she started wondering what she was still doing with him. They'd lost their spark a long time ago and had just been coasting these past few years. He wasn't supportive and he never made an effort with anything. Was he the one thing holding her back from achieving her dreams?

She felt a harrowing resentment at so many lost opportunities all because of him. She knew what she was doing was underhand, but caring about everyone else hadn't gotten her very far and she was struggling to visualise a future that Jamie was part of.

CHAPTER 10

The rest of the weekend was uneventful and Jane was glad to be back in the office. Monday mornings consisted mainly of catching up with emails, most of which were from lonely drunken people begging for help. All of which were a complete waste of time, but it was a great way to ease herself back into the working week.

Compiling her ever growing 'to do' list she added that she needed to call Andrew. Thinking about him took her mind back to the newspaper. It was a pretty pointless article, a young pretty blonde bragging about her one night with 'Mr Wonderful'. He had apparently left her stranded after having his wicked way with her. The article had so many holes it was hard to think people would actually believe it. Firstly how they met, and secondly how she ended up in a seedy hotel with him. She was fairly sure two people didn't just meet on the street and run off to have sex ….Well, not two strangers anyway. A pink blush crept across her cheeks, she wished her emotions weren't so visible these days.

Jane started to ponder on how far she'd let him go with his fake name charade before letting on that she knew exactly who he was.
Ring Ring…. Ring Ring

Checking the clock, Jane wondered who could be calling so early.

"Good morning Love Games, Jane speaking how can I help you?"

The moment she heard the voice she groaned in despair.

"Jane darling, I was going to call you yesterday but thought you may have been at your mothers." Joanna, off on the mother thing again. *Just humour her,* she thought, *and get her off the phone as quickly as you can.*

"No I actually went to Libby's Mum and Dad's, they invited us a few weeks back so we headed over there. What can I do for you?" She wasn't lying. This dinner had been on the calendar for weeks now and despite the two day hangover, she'd really been looking forward to it. Libby's mum cooked the best dinners ever. They hadn't called it her legendary roast for nothing.

"Oh, I will let you off then dear. So how was Friday?" *Wow! Get straight to the point why don't you.* she didn't want to be rude but this was borderline stalking. Pretty sure she had in fact left it that she would contact, she was a tad annoyed to be hearing from her first thing on a Monday morning when there was still a trace of the hangover left in her system.

"Well it wasn't the best but I will be seeing him again." Still not technically a lie. Ok, so they weren't going to be falling madly in love with each other any time soon, but they were going to be hanging out as friends. Point one for Jane.

"Well that is a shame……for Neil that is. Jane are you sure I can't tempt you to just have a drink with him? I really think you would like him dear." She was pushing and she should've just admitted defeat there and then, she didn't have the energy for this first thing in the morning.

"I could set something up for this evening if you are free?" Panicking, she racked her brains for any excuse as to why she wouldn't be able to meet him, but she couldn't think of one. *Why has my brain chosen to fail me now?* Her eyes were drawn to the light on her phone, indicating she had a new message.
It was Ben.
Hey Jane hope your head has stopped pounding, wanna go for a few drinks tonight?
Thank god! She screamed in her head. Saved by a text.

"Actually Joanna I have plans with Ben this evening so won't be able to. How about I get in touch with you when I have some spare time? I have loads on at the moment." But Joanna was too quick for her.

"I thought as much. Where will you be going? I can have Neil pop along just to say hi. You really ought to meet him my love." Sensing she wasn't going to be allowed to get her own way and really just wanting to get her off her case, she reluctantly agreed to send her the details of where they were going so she could meet this Neil guy.

Finishing her call she clicked out of the text message from Ben. *Oh, that's weird!* She'd noticed an unopened message on her phone from Saturday. Wondering why she hadn't seen it before now she clicked it open, it was from Andrew.
Jane, I want you!

Is that it? He's keen, she thought back to the answer message he'd left her on Friday saying pretty much the exact same thing. Jane didn't think there was much to it, other than he was clearly eager to get started with the process.

This morning, her most important job was to sort out this mess with Dean. Then she would be free to sort out seeing Ben.

"Morning." Libby chirped as she skipped into the office.

"Coffee shop was a nightmare, massive queues which resulted in blueberry muffins leaping into my hands. Want one?" Grinning, she motioned to the bag which clearly contained more than just two muffins.

"Sure, thanks. But what else did you get?" She noticed the bulging bag clutched in her hands.

"Erm……just a few snacks for the day." She was biting her lip which only meant one thing, she was trying to avoid telling.

"Ok I won't ask, just don't eat it all today else you will be moaning later that you need to lose weight. Not that you have ever had to worry about that. It sickens me!" It was true, Libby had the best metabolism ever and could literally eat whatever she wanted without gaining so much as half a pound. She however did have to work to keep her figure and it was always annoying to see Libby eating anything and everything and still remain svelte and petite.

"Hey, we haven't really been out for ages, fancy coming for a few drinks after work? Jamie should come too as you haven't seen him all weekend. How come he didn't make it to your folks yesterday?" It was the perfect plan. All of them going out for drinks. That way when she had to fulfil her duty and meet this Neil, Ben would have some company. She thought Libby and him would get on well seeing as they were both into their fashion.

"Oh he was busy. Yeah I can ask him. It would be nice for the three of us to hang out, it has been a while hasn't it?"

"Oh there will be four hun, we can have our girly chats while Jamie keeps Ben company."

She smiled, it sounded like it was going to be a great start to the week and she was really looking forward to it, well all apart from the meeting Neil part, but you can't have it all can you?

The colour had drained from Libby's face and Jane looked at her concerned.

"Are you alright hun?"

"Yeah, just thinking about something that's all." She reached down to pull her phone out of her bag under the table and discreetly typed out a text before Jane noticed.

Hi it's Libby the crazy flatmate of Jane's who left you the voicemail the other day. Can I just ask that you please don't say I called you and especially don't mention what it was about. Thank you

As she hit send the only thing going round in her head was, *this is going to be a total disaster!* That was until she got the reply she'd been waiting since Saturday for.

Hey sorry I was meaning to call you back. No worries I won't say anything to Jane. We should get together so we can talk properly.

Phew!! So maybe tonight isn't going to be that bad after all.

CHAPTER 11

"Aaarghh, I can't see what the mess up could possibly have been with Dean. I'm so angry with myself, it looks like I genuinely just fucked up." Jane was searching through files to see where a mistake could have occurred. From what she could see everything had been done according to her own protocol. How did she get it so wrong? The worst thing was that she didn't seem to have anyone currently on the books that would be remotely suitable for him.

"Calm down Jane, stressing isn't going to do you any good is it? Have you thought about poaching from other agencies or even going online? I know you would lose out on revenue but it could stop a bad review." Libby had mentioned this a couple of times before and most agencies did indeed outsource clients from other companies, but it was something that she'd never wanted to do for fear she'd end up relying on it. Also the impact on her profit margin was less than desirable.

If she couldn't find anyone to match with Dean though, she would have to seriously consider it, something she wasn't happy about. She hated not having control and it felt like things were starting to spiral.

"Give me a couple of days to see if I can find anyone. If I can't then you can have a look into it for me?"

"Jeez, you don't have to have a face about it, it's business babe that's all." But to her the business wasn't just work. It was, and always would be, her baby. Her whole life, and the feeling she was failing was like a mother watching her child fail knowing that they'd done everything they could to help them succeed, but it just not being enough.

"I have a couple of calls to make so do you want to crack on with some background research for me?" She went back to her list already knowing that the next most important thing on it was to call Andrew.

***

Working hard organising ideas for a new event had Andrew hunched over his desk, punching away furiously on his computer. Spread out in front of him were countless colour schemes, and at a push, some themed ideas. He hated doing them, but they were popular these days so had no choice but to offer them.

He had a meeting later that day with what could be one of his biggest clients to date, and he wanted to go through as many designs as he could to show how much work he was willing to do on their project should they go with Signature Events.

He was also in the process of buying yet another company that was drastically failing. This meant even longer hours than usual and even less downtime. It was something any prospective partner would have to be okay with as he didn't see his working pattern changing any time soon, if anything he would continue to grow his empire, the harder he worked the more alive he felt.

He'd often been referred to as Richard Gere's character in Pretty Woman, there were even the alleged prostitute stories too. Despite none of them being true, he'd always liked that film and the comparison didn't offend him. He liked helping and he always made sure to keep the previous owners for the day to day running. After all, they knew the business better than anyone, he just made changes to make it successful again.

The red light was flashing on his phone so he was forced to prize himself away from working to answer it. He knew it would be important as he'd told Rebecca he wasn't taking any calls that morning, he had far too much to do to be interrupted.

"Rebecca, what is it?" He hoped she just wanted to take his coffee order. He really fancied a strong one to help him to get through this proposal.

"Sorry to interrupt you Mr Blake but I have Jane from Love Games on the phone and I had a feeling you might want to take it..... I can always ask her to call back another time if it's inconvenient?"

"NO! Put her through right away!" Realising he'd just lost control. He didn't want anyone to know about his feelings. He spoke again quickly before she was able to say anything about it, She was a smart girl she was sure to have picked up on his eagerness.

"Thank you Rebecca." He was nervous, knowing that the only form of communication he'd had with Jane was through messages, either voicemail or text. Knowing she was waiting to be put through to him made him feel ridiculously on edge.

His heart was racing and he had sweat beading along his forehead. He had to remember he was Andrew Smith, an insurance manager looking for love. He was not Andrew Blake, totally infatuated by the woman on the other end of the phone.

He couldn't concentrate.

He just sat motionless for what seemed like an hour waiting for the phone to ring so he could answer the connected call.

Finally he heard the familiar sound and had to stop himself from picking it up after the first ring.

"Hello Andrew…..Smith here. Jane I believe?" *Ok tick one for remembering the name and tick two for remaining calm.* Despite feeling each beat of his heart as if it were trying to burst out of his chest he wasn't doing too badly. *You can do this Andrew.*

"Yes, Mr, ah, Smith it's Jane calling from Love Games. You left me a couple of messages telling me you wished to be put on our books. I am just calling to set up our next meeting."

"Are you free tomorrow?" He hadn't even let her finish talking. He knew today was out of the question, he had to get this proposal finished. He was seriously contemplating asking someone else to pitch to the client tomorrow if she was free to meet him.

"I actually have the day booked off tomorrow so that won't be any good for me. How about Wednesday? I currently have a clear diary that day, is there a time that suits you best?"

"9am, my office?" *Shit,* he thought, *I sound desperate don't I? I must sound like an idiot. I haven't even checked my schedule to see if I can do Wednesday, but it really doesn't matter if she can.* He just knew he had to see her again soon, and this need was taking over his common senses.

".Oh, I was expecting you to say something around lunchtime like before but sure I will pop you in the diary for Wednesday at 9am, can you email me the address? I am sure we won't have any issues finding someone for you."

Of course, she was going to be setting him up on dates with *other people*. In all the rush to make sure he was able to see her again he'd forgotten she was there to find him someone. Surely there couldn't be anyone else out there that made him feel the way she did. He half hoped that when he saw her again he would find it had all been just fantasy and he'd imagined the feelings that had taken over his senses since Friday.

The fact was he hadn't been able to focus on anything all weekend except her face, something his erotic dreams hadn't helped with either. Every time he thought about them he got hard and it took him forever to regain any form of control over himself. Perhaps he just needed one night with her, you know, to get her out of his system so to speak. The issue was that she was now technically employed by him, he was going to be paying for her service. If he were to sleep with her then wouldn't that make the references to Pretty Woman true? He would have basically paid for sex. He really didn't like that idea.

He had to think about this.

He had to get it right and he had until Wednesday to work out how to do it.

CHAPTER 12

Jane was thankful to close her laptop at the end of a long and extremely unsuccessful day. The search for Dean's perfect match had ground to a miserable halt. She didn't want to admit it but Libby was right, now may be the time to outsource. Deciding she would try again on Wednesday before admitting defeat she thought it would be a good idea to network this evening and try and get some new names added to the books.

After five years of success this day was always inevitable. Even though she knew it would come, she had hoped to be riding the waves of success for a little while longer. Libby had left early to go home and get ready, she would never be seen dead going out in what she'd been wearing at work. They'd arranged to meet at their favourite bar once she let her know she had locked up and was on her way. That was the good thing about London, you could get everywhere reasonably quick thanks to the underground. She did have a car, but why drive when this was so convenient She popped Libby a text before heading into the station, if she left it too late she would never get reception once on the train.

Never before had she been so thankful to leave the confines of her office. It helped knowing she wouldn't be back there tomorrow. Having booked the day off to go and see her Mum she now found she was really looking forward to it. She needed the break and she needed her mum. But that was tomorrow, tonight there were cocktails with her name written all over them.

Ben was already waiting when she arrived but there was no sign of Libby or Jamie.

"Ben, hi you ok?" She greeted him with a hug like he was an old friend.

"Yeah good thanks, been working on an underwear shoot all day so it's nice to have some clothes on." His smile gave off a warmth that made her feel happy for the first time that day.

"I hope you don't mind but I invited Libby and Jamie along as it's been like forever since we all hung out and I thought it would be good for you to meet them. I live with Libby actually, she was the one asleep when you kindly saved me last week."

She really liked Ben, he made her feel safe and happy. She could see him as her big brother type friend. The one that would let her cry on his shoulder when she needed to, the one that would fight to defend her if needed, but also the one that wouldn't expect anything other than friendship in return. She hadn't realised she needed someone like him. Libby was great, the best even, but having a male BFF is brilliant. They can put things into perspective from a man's point of view and lets face it men are such a strange species, we need all the help we can get.

"No that's great, the more the merrier. Shall we?" Ben motioned towards the door.

"Sure but the first round is on me so quick, hurry up and order before the others get here!"

Quickly pushing open the door they walked into the bar arm in arm, laughing, they ordered their drinks before grabbing a seat by the window. They were deep in conversation when Jamie arrived.

Jane was surprised he hadn't arranged to meet Libby before coming, she caught his eye and waved, letting him know where they were.

"Hi Jane." He smiled weakly at her before quickly turning to Ben. He looked relieved to have someone else to talk to.

"Hi i'm Jamie, you are?"

"This is Ben, we went out on Friday." He didn't even turn to look at her as she explained to him. He just leant forward to shake Ben's hand before sliding into the chair next to him completely avoiding eye contact with her. Not wanting to make a scene or make Ben uncomfortable she decided to bite her tongue, now wasn't the time or the place. If Libby caught him being that way with her then there would be hell to pay for sure. She could hold off until then to get her own back.

Another thirty, uncomfortable, minutes passed before Libby eventually arrived. Thirty minutes where she struggled to contribute to the conversation. Ben and Jamie were deep in discussion about the games that Jamie worked on and clearly Ben felt he was an expert on. Still, Jane was happy they were getting along.

Libby looked incredible, she'd never seen the outfit she was wearing before and she wanted one.

"Oh Libby wow, you look....just wow! Where did you get this?"

"Oh this old thing. I've had it for a while, just haven't had the chance to crack it out and give it a test drive. I, err, actually I designed it myself."

"But how come it's made up? Have you taken up sewing without me noticing? You aren't usually the secretive type, what gives?"

"No, nothing like that. I found an incredibly talented seamstress to make it up for me. So, it's a one off at the moment so don't even try squeezing into it!" Libby looked embarrassed and tried to move the conversation off her fabulous attire.

It was the reason why she was always skint, she had been paying the seamstress instalments every month to make up a collection of her work. That way when she made appointments with prospective employers, she could not only show them her drawings but could model the pieces first hand. Things always looked better once made up and her petite figure had a way of making anything look good.

"Hi, you must be Ben." Libby warily glanced over at him.

"And you must be the famous sofa sleeping Libby." He grinned at her and gave her a sly wink to show that his lips were sealed.

"Wait. Have I missed something? Have you two met before?" Jamie narrowed his eyes and looked from Ben to Libby and back again, looking for any sign that they were hiding something.

"Not quite." Ben was grinning again, making Libby blush and Jamie got even more agitated. His eyes, barely visible through the narrow slits surrounding them.

"Well I did my usual ritual of waiting up for Jane after her date but fell asleep on the sofa. So when she let Ben out on Saturday morning he kind of saw me snoring away on the sofa. So embarrassing!"

"Oh, but I thought you two were just friends? Another notch on the bedpost first hey Jane?" She looked like she'd been slapped in the face and was about to explode but Libby and Ben were on the case before she had chance to even open her mouth.

"No, nothing like that mate." Jamie wasn't happy, he looked like he was ready to kill, both Ben and Libby could sense the bomb that was about to explode.

"Actually he helped her home after she was far too drunk to make any decent decisions for herself. He looked after her so she didn't disturb moi." His expression told them he didn't buy any of it but didn't say anything more, just sat glaring out the window.

The good feelings Jane had melted away and a need to forget surfaced once again. Downing her cocktail she motioned to Libby she was heading to the bar. She saw that everyone else was still nursing their first drinks so didn't bother asking if anyone wanted another. She knew she needed to hit it hard again. She also knew it was out of character but the way things had been turning out recently there was nothing she wanted more than the sweet elixir that was alcohol.

They passed the next couple of hours away quite happily, the drinks flowed nicely which matched the conversation and Jane was glad Ben was getting on with everyone so well. He was a breath of fresh air for the group and she was thankful he was there because it kept Jamie from making any more snide remarks about her. Still reeling from the one he made earlier, she was about to take another gulp of her drink when she noticed someone standing at the bar staring at her.

At first she wondered if he really was looking at her so she looked around to see if there was anyone in her vicinity he could really be staring so intently at. There was no-one even remotely close and seeing as they were in the window seats, it couldn't very well be anyone behind her. To her dismay she saw that Libby had noticed him too.

"Oh look Jane has pulled already!" Everybody looked at the man who hastily turned back towards the bar. Jane didn't blame him. She felt a bit sorry for him. How awful to have a group of people noticing his weird actions and pointing them out to everyone else in the pub. Perhaps he knew of her through work? Thinking she had lost a potential new client she found herself getting annoyed with Libby.

"Lib that was mean, I'm going to see if he is alright." Sliding out of her seat she started walking towards the strange man at the bar, taking in his appearance with every step she took.

Overall he didn't look that bad, but clearly wasn't a competent dresser. The suit he was wearing didn't match, and didn't really fit him all that well either. He was skinny and not very tall and it looked like a hand-me-down which he didn't know to have tailored so that it actually fit.

Having been on the other side of the room she hadn't been able to make out his face, he could be a real lost cause. The closer she got to him the more she found he wasn't too bad. He had a beautiful jawline and cheekbones any model would die for, sandy coloured hair that was a tad unkempt, but the style suited him. He was the epitome of geek chic.

Jane made it to the bar and stood next to him, only he still hadn't realised she was there. Clearing her throat to try and get his attention she turned herself towards him.

"Erm, hi. I just wanted to apologise for my friend over there. We've been here a little while so are all feeling a tad tipsy." He looked up and smiled, she took that to mean that he was alright.

"Jane, sorry to stare at you, but I was trying to gauge the perfect time to steal a few minutes alone with you."

"How do you know my name?" She was confused. Trying to figure out if she knew him when it dawned on her.

"Neil! Oh my god I am so sorry! I totally forgot I was meeting you."

"No harm done, my tactics worked didn't they? Got you over here talking to me. I must say you are much better looking than Joanna described."

"Well Joanna has trouble praising anything doesn't she!" Remembering that he worked with Joanna, she regretted letting the remark slip out.

"Actually, the only thing she's ever spoken highly of is you Neil. You have a very big reputation to live up to now."

They stood talking for a little while before she noticed Libby staring at them. She looked like she was just about to make some remark to the boys when Jane shook her head at her, pleading at her to leave it alone.

"Neil, as lovely as this is I have to get back to my friends else they will send out a search party for me."

"Oh I'm sorry to keep you. It would be nice to see you again. Here is my number, you should give me a call when you have more time."

She thought about it, he wasn't her type at all and he had zero fashion sense. You really wouldn't look at him twice if you were in a crowded room, but he seemed kind and was very interested in what she had to say, unlike most men who were only interested in what was in her pants, so she reached out to take his card. She had a feeling she'd be seeing him again.

"Thanks. It was lovely meeting you. And sorry again for my friend." She began walking back to her table but stopped to throw a cheeky look back at him. He was leaning on the bar watching her go, a grin plastered on his face. *Shit, he wasn't supposed to be looking at me! He seemed nice, maybe I should go on a date with him...* she thought. Then an image of a smug Joanna flashed into her head causing bile to rise up her throat and make it burn. The thought of pleasing Joanna was sickening and she pushed his card to the bottom of her bag. Maybe it wasn't such a good idea after all.

She hadn't noticed Ben leave to get more drinks but he returned to the table with their next round and what appeared to be shots for each of them too Jane downed her shot and took a huge swig of her drink to help rid herself of the image and push the bile back down where it should be.

"Hey, I know, why don't we go on to a club? I am in the mood for dancing and Libby is far too hot in that outfit to be going home before midnight." She was usually the sensible one who opted for an early night, not the party animal that she was coming across as so she knew the alcohol had kicked in.

"Well as my Nolan sister over there rightly put it, I'm in the mood for dancing too, lets get it on guys!" Jane burst into a fit of laughter as Libby sang the words of the popular song she hadn't realised she'd even quoted. Libby was giggling too and it took a while before either of them could speak while the boys just sat waiting patiently for them to calm down. Ben found their outburst humorous but Jamie just turned sour again.

"Lib, babe, I have work tomorrow, don't you think we should just head off after this and give clubbing a miss?" Jamie detested clubs, it was a well known fact. He hated the loud music. He hated the price it cost you to get in. He hated the cost of the drinks once you were finally inside. And he hated how crowded they always were, even on a Monday night. It was London after all.

"Oh Jamie just live a little will you. You never know it might help spice things up a bit!" She spat back at him.

"What's that meant to mean? I just don't think it's wise to be drinking all night when everyone has work tomorrow that's all. Plus you know I don't like clubs, anyone would think you were deliberately trying to piss me off." If Libby erupted now there would be no survivors and he was well aware of this fact, but he was seriously pissed off and couldn't help show it in the way he spoke to her.

"I can get us all into Marilyn's if you fancy it, my name is usually on the guest list when they know |'m in town." Ben used the pause as the perfect opportunity to make a suggestion.

"MARILYN'S!!" The girls screeched at exactly the same time, both had wide eyes and huge grins.

Marilyn's. The exclusive club where you had to *'be somebody'* to get in. It had been both the girls dream to be successful enough to one day go there. They jumped on him at the same time, throwing their arms around him and kissing his cheeks taking him by surprise while Jamie looked on sullenly.

"Shall I take that as a yes?" He asked laughing at their reaction.

~

Arriving outside the main entrance of the club Jane and Libby were literally beside themselves with excitement. Tottering up to the bouncer each arm linked through Ben's while Jamie trudged behind, they were all let in as soon as Ben mentioned his name and flashed his pearly white grin.

"Good to see you again Benjamin." The doorman moved aside to let them all in. Inside was better than anything the girls ever dreamed it would be. It had the most amazing decor and intricate chandelier's hung from the ceiling down the corridor which led them to the first of, what they would soon find out to be, many rooms. The door they were about to go through told them they were heading for the Main Room. Jane felt a rush of excitement as she wondered what they were about to see behind it.

The lighting was dim and there were lots of plush, comfortable chairs around small glass tables with the kind of centrepieces you would expect to find at a celebrity wedding not inside a club. It was intimate and seriously intense. They stood mesmerised for a moment when, at the exact same time, they noticed the little corner stage at the other end of the room.

On it a sleek silver pole had been erected from floor to ceiling. They looked at one another mouthing *'Oh my god!!'* Tearing their eyes away from the empty stage they continued to look around the room, taking it all in.

The bar was made of glass and full of water containing the most exotic fish they'd ever seen. The lights within the bar changed every few seconds from blues, to reds to greens in such a soft way, you could be mesmerised by that alone, well until the dancers came out anyway.

The wall behind the bar was full of shelves, each one containing row after row of crystal glasses in all shapes and sizes. She wished she knew what each glass was meant for but in their lifestyle if you ran out of glasses you just drank your wine from a coffee mug. She felt very out of her depth and it made her nervous, she didn't want to show Ben up, she fully intended to come here again with him.

There were a few other doors leading into other areas of the club. She wanted to rush around and see what they all were but knew she had to contain her excitement and make sure she didn't embarrass Ben. Even Jamie looked impressed with the place. She'd noticed his eyes widen when he walked in and even detected the hint of a smile when he clocked the pole. Maybe he wouldn't be such a grumpy git after all.

Ben led them over to the bar and nodded at the barman who then commenced pouring out four glasses of champagne. No money exchanged hands and an impeccably dressed woman came out with a silver tray to carry them over to their table for them. They followed her over to a corner booth that had the perfect view of the whole room. She didn't say a word to any of them but nodded to Ben, smiled at them all, and then walked away.

"Libby how good is this?! I feel like a celebrity!" It'd been the first time Jane felt she could vocally express how she felt about the place since they arrived, and Libby agreed. The grin on her face literally reached from one ear to the other and she wasn't able to put into words how she was feeling. It took a lot to render her speechless but this place had managed it. She simply sat, wide eyed, with a huge cheshire cat kind of smile as her eyes scanned the room yet again.

Taking a moment to see who else was there, she noticed some familiar faces. Footballers, footballers wives, TV favourites, you name it they were here. This was obviously a popular hang out for a lot of people, they all looked so relaxed, the complete opposite of how she felt.

She watched as a door opened to their left and a couple of women walked in. They were ridiculously tall even without the six inch heels they were teetering on top of. One wore a black and pink frilly basque with fishnet stockings and lacy suspender belt, the other was sporting a pink satin robe with a furry edging and lord knows what underneath. *Ahh, so these must be the dancers.* They looked like they would be able to wrap those legs around the pole several times over. She was looking forward to the show starting, along with many of the other people in the room who had now started looking towards the stage.

As if reading her thoughts, the woman in the basque mounted it and gave a thumbs up to a stranger Jane wasn't able see. The music changed and a provocative instrumental filled the room, increasing in volume indicating the show was about to begin.

Taking the opportunity to empty her glass, she found she was starting to feel heady from the alcohol. She knew she should start pacing herself, but before she had chance to place her glass back down, the little woman from earlier was there with a full one to replace it. *I could get used to this.*

She told herself to make the most of tonight, she would try to experience as much Marilyn's had to offer as who knows when Ben would be back in London again? Taking a sip of her fresh drink she turned to enjoy the show.

CHAPTER 13

"Oh em gee, that was so hot! If Jamie wasn't being such a prick I might have jumped him there and then." They giddily made their way to the bathroom once the dancers left the stage. Pushing open the door, Jane stopped to take stock of what was before her.

"Bloody hell, this bathroom is bigger than our flipping flat!" Libby pushed her aside and ran inside throwing her arms wide and started spinning around like a child being set free for the first time.

"Holy shit. How is that fair? We pay a small fortune for our shoe box and the rich and famous get this as a bathroom on a night out!" They burst out laughing as she continued to run around like a lunatic. They eventually composed themselves and began the mammoth task of re-applying their lipstick. In their drunken state it was as tricky a task as diffusing a bomb would be, a highly stressful manoeuvre, one slip of the hand and....Boom! Catastrophe.

"As much as you moan about him, at least you have the option of going home with someone at the end of the night. Tonight I will mostly be making love to these." Holding up her right hand she wiggled her fingers and they burst into fits of giggles again, only stopping when the door opened and someone walked in.

The woman smiled at them but had narrowed her eyes, almost as if she was trying to figure out who they were and if they should be there or not. Not wanting to stay too long and make it obvious she continued into a nearby cubicle, slowly closing the door behind her giving her a bit longer to suss them out.

They both had trouble composing themselves but didn't want the woman to think she was being laughed at. They pushed clumsily back into the corridor. Unable to hold it in any longer they proceeded to fall about on the floor. *Laughter really is the best medicine,* Jane thought, *well laughter and champagne, but they kind of go hand in hand really don't they?*

Walking back into the Main Room she stopped in her tracks, not believing it could be she desperately tried to get her eyes to focus. Grabbing Libby's arm to stop her from walking away, she whispered in her ear as discreetly as she could manage.

"Libby, look that's him isn't it? That's Andrew Blake." She wanted confirmation that she had indeed got the right person before making a total fool of herself.

"Oh wow yeah, looks like it. I heard he owned this place now but didn't expect him to actually be here." Libby didn't get it, of course she didn't, *I haven't told her about the whole Andrew Smith escapade yet have I?*

"No, you don't understand! That's the man I met with on Friday. The one that left that message at work. The one I called back today. That is Andrew Smith."

"Er, Jane, I think you have had a bit too much to drink dear. That beautiful specimen of a man is Andrew Blake. The very famous and, it would appear, very hot, Andrew Blake. I didn't realise he was so good looking did you? Come on, the boys are waiting." She started to walk away but Jane was rooted to the spot.

Just at that moment he turned around, his ice blue eyes locking on hers just as they had on Friday, the whole club seemed to melt away around them. It was just him and her and she could feel him drawing her in. Without realising she was even moving her feet carried her towards him, each step as if she was floating, she was moving without any control from her brain which was now screaming at them to STOP!

It wasn't until she saw the lady from the bathroom returning to her seat, which happened to be right next to him, that she changed course and headed back to her own table. Feeling her face burn hot with sheer embarrassment she finished what was left in her glass. As if on cue another was placed in front of her.

Not daring to look up in-case he was still watching her after her odd behaviour, Libby came to her rescue.

"I thought we were going to do some dancing guys! Ben, what's the best room to get our groove on?" *Yes,* she thought, *anything to get me out of this room!*

"The Dance room. It has a great DJ in there."

"Settled then, Jane c'mon." She jumped up dragging her off her seat and they both headed towards the Dance room, she tried to only focus on their destination and nothing else, so was shocked when an arm came out in front of them stopping their entry.

About to protest she looked up, ready to argue. *Oh god, those eyes!* Her insides melted and her breathing became raspy. She was dizzy and she couldn't work out if it was because of him or the alcohol.

"Excuse me, Mr Smith is it? We were actually about to go in there. Was there something we could do for you?" She was thankful her voice wasn't reflecting how she really felt. She was intimidated by him but wasn't sure why. Her clipped tone made her sound powerful, hearing it gave her the confidence to keep talking. She had to remember he was *still* her client, despite his lies.

"Apologies Jane, I just wanted to make sure you were alright, you looked like you were going to come over, but then when I looked back you'd gone?"

"I didn't want to disturb you on your date. Speaking of that, could you tell me why you even need my help? It seems the famous Mr *Blake* has no problems finding women. From what I have read recently and from what I have seen tonight you don't need me at all." With an air of disgust in her voice, she realised how ironic it was that she was looking down her nose at his bedroom antics after what she'd done recently.

"Ahh, that." His eyes lingered on the floor for a while before looking straight into hers. She wished he would stop doing that, he was practically hypnotising her just by making eye contact.

"Er, Hi. I'm Libby, Jane's dance partner for the evening and we have a date with that particular dance floor in there. If this is work talk, can you not keep it for your appointment on Wednesday?" She pushed past them both and walked into the room, pausing to hold the door open for Jane to follow. A stern look told her she should go with her. She knew she should, but she couldn't leave things with Andrew the way they were, not if she had to see him again that week.

"Give me a minute I will come find you Lib." Turning back to him she continued.

"Mr Smith, Blake whatever it is you are choosing to call yourself today, I apologise for acting unprofessionally. If you still wish to keep the meeting then I will see you on Wednesday." He leant in so close that they were almost touching.
She could feel the heat from his breath on her face.
He was so close she was able to smell the sweet liquor staining his breath each time he exhaled.
His sheer proximity was turning her on and she closed her eyes willing him to kiss her.

He moved his mouth towards her ear, his lips gently brushing her cheek as they found their way to their destination. It made every nerve in her body stand to attention. Swallowing hard, she wasn't sure what to expect next. He was either going to kiss her or whisper something? Her whole body was silently screaming at him *KISS ME* while her brain, the only rational part of her body, albeit slightly sozzled, was wondering *why do you want this?*

"I want you!" Those three words again, simple but so powerful that they made her core physically ache for him. Opening her eyes she could see him walking away from her. Was she supposed to follow? Looking around she noticed the lady he'd been sitting with looking over at her but quickly shifting her gaze once she saw she'd been spotted.

She knew she shouldn't but couldn't stop herself from following. He took her down a corridor, one that didn't look like it led anywhere. He stopped and simply stood with his back to her. When he heard her approach he span around. She continued walking towards him, not knowing what was going to happen next, the adrenaline and curiosity spurring her on. She was overcome with a sense of control and she had one thing on her mind....him.

She stopped in front of him. Neither said a word. He lifted his hands and gently placed them on her cheeks, feeling his warmth and tenderness as each finger traced her jawline. Not taking their eyes off each other the electricity sparked around them. This was a whole new sensation for her and she felt like she was about to have her first ever kiss all over again.

Licking her lips, the mere smell of him had her intoxicated. The only thing she was sure of right now was that she wanted more. She wanted to bottle it. The feeling that nothing else in the entire world mattered but each other. It was so intense it made her feel like a complete novice.

When she thought she couldn't wait any longer he pressed his lips down to meet hers. It was the most gentle kiss anyone had ever given her but she was hungry for passion. She pulled herself deeper into his embrace as he masterfully worked her mouth, darting his tongue in and out in such a way it made her legs shake. She'd never been kissed like this before and for a split second she felt overwhelmed and pulled away. Andrew stiffened and his face became grave.

"Jane, I am sorry. I should never have...." He turned on his heel and marched back down the corridor back towards the bar. She couldn't follow. Her body was numb, all the blood seemingly in her plumped lips which were throbbing from their passionate embrace. Raising a finger she traced it along her bottom lip, remembering how good it had felt when his lips had been there. She was left feeling confused, why had he left her? *What does it mean?*

***

"Shit" Andrew cursed as he barged back into the bar. *How could I have been so stupid?* He'd only taken her out there to explain about his facade as Mr Smith and to make sure their appointment on Wednesday was still on. Now he'd be lucky if she ever returned any of his calls. *How could I have let that happen?*

"Oi, mate. Where's Jane? What have you done with her? Is she ok?" *Who is this clown?* He thought angrily. He'd done his research, he knew she was single so who did this jackass think he was. Ignoring him he carried on walking, he didn't have to answer to anyone, this was his club, *his,* and he could do what he damn well wanted in it.

"Oi, I am talking to you!"

He's not going to give up is he? Spinning around he saw the dark haired guy Jane had been sitting with stalking towards him. *Ok, yeah so you're well built but I have eyes all around this place so just try it.* 'When he'd gotten closer the man spoke to him yet again.

"Did you not hear me or something? Where is she? I saw her leave with you and she hasn't come back?"

"I don't think it's any of your business, but Jane was fine when I left her."

"I'm her friend so that makes it my business. Why hasn't she come back? What did you do to her?" *Why hasn't she come back?* Andrew wondered. *Is she ok?* He'd been so annoyed with his own actions he hadn't stopped to see how *she* was. *She pulled away from you, that means she didn't want you.* Her kiss had said differently, but ultimately she was the one to back away. He was old enough to be able to read the signals by now.

He needed to get out, needed to feel fresh air on his skin, to have it invigorate his senses so he was able to think clearer. What he really wanted was to speak to Jane.

With this final thought he turned his back on Ben and started to walk towards the exit, at the same time reaching in his pocket for his phone. He was about to text her to ask if he could speak to her tomorrow when they'd sobered up when…

BANG

The first blow connected with the back of his head, knocking him to the floor.

BANG

The second punch only just made contact. He was sure it was because his bodyguards had raced to the scene to help.

BANG

Another blow found it's way directly to his head. That was when he heard the scream.

"Nooooo!"

There were rushing noises and the sound of feet running towards him.

"What the hell do you think you are doing?" *Jane!!* He wanted to shout out to her. He could hear people filing out of all the doors around him but was unable to move off the floor.

"What the hell has happened?"

"What's going on?"

"Who is on the floor?"

"Andrew Blake?"

"What were you thinking?"

Still not aware of what was going on around him or how bad the situation actually was just hearing all the cries and shouts of people around him, but unable to make out who was actually speaking. It all blurred into one, he closed his eyes to shut out the noise. Then everything went dark.

CHAPTER 14

"Mum stop fussing, I'm ok." Jane took another slice of toast from the rack and poured herself a coffee from the steaming pot. Seating herself at the dining table she tightened her robe and stared out into the conservatory. Despite the events that led to her arriving at her parents house in the early hours of the morning in the back of a police car, she was thankful to be there.

Jane had always adored her family home, having never lived anywhere else until she left to go to university, it always would hold a fond place in her heart. So many childhood memories had been captured within the walls and she always felt safe whenever she was there. Sipping her coffee she gazed out at the sunshine beating down in the garden, she wished she could stay there forever.

"Jane my love we really do need to know what happened. The police just said there had been an altercation and you were helping with their enquiries." Her mother placed a hand on top of hers. She was stunned at its appearance and just stared at it for a few moments, noticing the skin was crinkled more than ever and it looked paper thin, like the slightest movement would cause it to rip. There was evidence of age spots starting to appear and her fingers seemed to have gotten thinner, the rings she wore now fell to one side. She thought it would just take one swift gesture and they would fly off entirely. In the blink of an eye her parents had gotten old. They were winding down their lives now, taking things at a more leisurely pace and they sure as hell didn't need her bringing this kind of shit to their doorstep. She wasn't a teenager anymore and had to deal with this herself.

"It was all a misunderstanding really, a friend of ours, Ben, got the wrong idea about a guy and there was a fight…..Well actually Ben was the only one that threw any punches so I guess that would be an attack in the eyes of the law. It was horrible…….he was just lying

there…" She felt the moisture tickle her cheek as a single tear escaped her eye. She felt numb every time she thought back to what had happened. Even though they'd assured her at the police station Andrew was fine, he'd just been knocked out, she still couldn't shake the image of him lying there.
Motionless.
Helpless.

There was then the shock that it'd been Ben that had done it. She hadn't stuck around to hear the ins and outs of it all, but gathered it was something to do with Andrew fooling around with his younger sister, promising her the world but never fulfilling it. She could understand why he would be pissed, but to do that? She knew she didn't really know Ben, what he was and wasn't capable of were all still unclear, but now she didn't know if she wanted to spend time with him and find any more out. This violent side of him was a deal breaker for her.

She watched her mother pour herself a coffee and take a croissant out of the bread bin before sitting back down next to her.

"Where's Dad?"

"He's gone to the golf club, thought it might be better for me to speak to you on your own. You know what he is like." She looked hard at her mother. She was impeccably dressed for that time of the day. Full face of make-up, a smart pant suit in lemon and a string of delicate pearls draped around her neck. Her hair was styled in its usual mid-length bob, not a single strand out of place. She thought back to the days where she would have to leave the room when her mother was getting ready as the half can of hairspray she used each day almost left her suffering an asthma attack. The memory made her smile, she wished she could return to those simpler times.

She was stunningly beautiful, even at her age she could still turn heads, but Jane could now make out the dark circles under her eyes, the sunken skin and despite how much she backcombed to get volume, she could see her mothers hair was thinning. It was cruel of the world to take something so beautiful and let it slowly wither and decay right in front of your eyes. She decided not to dwell on it else she would fall into a deep depression, one she would never get out of. Her parents still had plenty of life left in them so she would stop worrying until it was warranted.

"What are your plans for today then dear? It's your day off, we could go shopping, have lunch? How long are you staying for?"

"Lunch would be good, but I don't think I have the energy for shopping." All she needed was sleep and food and maybe even some uninterrupted sunshine out in the garden. Sitting out in the sunshine was a novelty once you'd lived in the centre of London in a flat for so long, she wanted to make the most of the opportunity.

Hearing her phone beeping deep within her bag that had been discarded on the kitchen counter, her mum rose to get it.

"It's ok mum, I will get it and then I might go back to bed for a bit. It was a late night." Grabbing her bag she walked out the kitchen and headed up the stairs until she reached her bedroom door.

Once safely inside she threw herself onto the bed and pulled out her phone. *Wow, it must have been going off all morning,* she found missed calls from Libby, texts from Ben and one message from an unknown number. Intrigued, she went to it first.

Jane I'm fine. Are you alright? A

It was him. Her heart was racing. She hadn't expected to hear from him ever again. Quickly hitting the reply button she typed.

I can't believe what happened, I am so sorry. J x

She looked at the message for several minutes, deleting then retyping, *kiss or no kiss? Kiss or no kiss?* Deciding to keep the kiss she hit send. Looking through her other messages wondering when or if she'd even get a response from him, she saw the ten texts from Ben. He must have gotten released shortly after they were all sent home.

Apologising in all of them and begging to speak to her so he could explain, but she wasn't sure she could face him yet so cancelled them all. She needed to get her head sorted and decide if she even wanted to hear more. She typed out one last text.

Libby, I'm ok hope you are. Speak to you later. J xxx

Then lay back on her plush pillow and fell into a much needed deep sleep. Knowing Andrew was alright seemed to have the calming effect she needed in order to drift off.

CHAPTER 15

Waking up to the sounds of her mother chatting away in the kitchen below, Jane felt a lot brighter and mustered some strength from somewhere to sit up. Wondering who her mum could be talking to if her dad was out playing golf, she wiped the sleep from her eyes and headed into the en-suite.

Once in the cubicle she immersed herself fully in the hot steamy water. This was what she needed, a good sleep, and a cleansing shower. Yes, she could have had both these at home but then she wouldn't have had the distraction of her mum to help take her mind off everything. No, here she could forget she was a grown up and go back to being a child and have someone look after her. Well for twenty four hours at least before reality would have to kick back in again.

Stepping out she caught the scent of freshly brewed coffee. The smell alone made her hurry with her dressing. Coffee was a necessity on a normal day, but with yet another hangover it was now an essential. Brushing on a small amount of powder and blusher over her tired pale skin she then quickly ran a brush through her hair before knotting it into a messy bun. She felt ready to head back downstairs. No doubt her mum would want to go out somewhere for lunch so wanted to be ready to go as soon as it was decided where. The noises coming from her stomach were making it clear she wasn't going to be able to wait long for sustenance.

It wasn't until she was nearing the bottom of the stairs she remembered that her mum wasn't alone. Hearing a familiar voice made her insides tighten into a knot and rendered her unable to move. If it hadn't been for her mother walking past at that very moment and ushering her into the kitchen, she would've tried to make her escape, either out the door or back up to her room, locking it firmly behind her until their ghastly house guest had gone.

"Morning Joanna." She said feebly. She knew all too well that Joanna was there for the story. She would've heard about what happened last night for sure and the fact that she'd been right there in the heart of all the action now made her Joanna's new best friend.

"Jane dear, good morning. I heard you had quite a night last night." *Not wasting any time are you?*

"I thought Joanna could join us for lunch, it's been a while since the three of us had any girly time." Her mother interjected but seeing her pained look she stopped. Joanna hadn't noticed the unspoken conversation going on between them. The pleading looks from Jane for her *not* to join them and the apologetic looks she got back that said, *it's too late.*

"Well that sounds like a grand idea mother." There was a harsh edge in her voice but again it went unnoticed, by Joanna at least. She was too busy setting her sights on getting the story so she could have another front page spread.

"Excellent, I have made reservations already." Joanna usually made plans in advance knowing she would get her own way in the end, both her and her mother had given up even trying to make excuses with her now.

"Of course you have." She muttered under her breath which earned her a filthy look off her mother.

A little while later they pulled up at the restaurant. It was a bit posh for a lunchtime but she thought if she didn't have to pay then who cares? Food is food at the end of the day and she needed some asap.

They were seated instantly and a complimentary bottle of wine was brought to the table. The thought of drinking it made her stomach flip and she had to close her mouth to stop herself from being sick. Food and coffee, that was all she wanted. Picking up the menu so she was ready to order as soon as the waitress came back, but the words all blurred into one. She must be a lot worse than she thought. How was she going to defend herself from Joanna when she wasn't at the top of her game?

Amazingly it wasn't until their food had been brought out before Joanna started with her tirade of questions. Jane was surprised she hadn't pulled out her notebook and pen to make sure she got it all down.

"So, Jane, tell me about last night?"

"Well I am sure you already know most of what happened. It was just a friend of mine, he got into a fight."

"So it was a friend of yours... Have you known him long? And how do you know Andrew Blake?"

"Ben, I haven't known long no."

"And Andrew?"

"Is an acquaintance through work."

"A source tells me that he took you off to a remote part of the club. Is that right? What did he want with you? Are you sure you don't know him other than through work?" She was squinting at her. Jane was glad that she didn't have the power to read her thoughts.

She sat staring at her fries not knowing how to answer. She couldn't reveal that he was a client of hers, he still was her client as far as she was aware. She realised that despite everything she wasn't sure if she'd cope not ever seeing him again. She had to know if it was true about Ben's sister but how could she find out without asking him outright?

He was sure to have a past, you couldn't be that good looking and not have a long dating history. But to lead someone on, promising them so much and then never speaking to them again, that was just evil. She needed to skip answering the last few questions, her brain couldn't formulate an answer to any of them, so she changed her tactics and brought up Neil.

"Oh yes in all the drama I had forgotten about your little meeting. He is a real gem isn't he?"

"He was alright actually yes. I'm not sure there was anything there though."

"What on earth do you mean? You only spoke to him for a short amount of time, how can you say there wasn't anything there? You must go on a proper date with him." This was the last thing she needed, another crappy date with a guy she didn't really feel anything for. It was like the universe was punishing her for all the bad choices she'd ever made.

"Oh Joanna is this the one you have been telling me about?" It'd been the first chance her mother had been able to join in with the conversation and she seemed relieved to finally be able to speak. She wasn't one for staying quiet, Jane wondered how her and Joanna had been friends for so long when they both liked to take centre stage in a conversation.

Off they both went gibbering away about how lovely Neil sounded, how perfect he seemed for her, almost as if she wasn't at the table with them. In a way she was thankful for the reprieve. Time to just be able to sit quietly eating her fries and daydream about Andrew. If there was an ounce of truth in any of the stories about him she should probably steer clear, yet all she wanted to do was go and see him and throw her arms around him and recreate that kiss all over again.

Confused by her feelings she figured there must be something wrong with her. This guy had been accused of being a total jerk on more than one occasion, so why were her sympathies with him? With her thoughts spinning round her head she pulled out her phone. She hadn't had anything back from him and she needed some contact with him.

Typing out a short message, she stopped and re-read it making sure it didn't sound desperate, scared that her kiss had frightened him off.

Are we still meeting tomorrow? I want to see you J x

      She was about to put her phone in her bag when she saw it flash up. It was from him. Eagerly she opened it.

9am tomorrow, my office A x

      Jane felt her heart flutter. He wanted to see her, all was not lost. Her eyes were drawn to the end of the message, he'd put a kiss. Without realising it she was smiling and for the first time in ages she felt hopeful. He'd kissed her last night and she felt something deep within her, something she couldn't describe no matter how hard she tried and he *still* wanted to see her. Thinking this could really be the start of something, she vowed not to let anything spoil her good feeling.

      "So it's agreed then, you will go on a proper date with him. That's great news I will have something set up for you both." It took a few moments for it to register that Joanna was talking to her. Three things popped into her head at the exact same time. *Why am I nodding? What have I just agreed to? What the fuck has just happened?*

CHAPTER 16

Jane woke at 5am the next morning. She was back at home, snuggled into her own bed. She'd been glad to get back home last night, Libby had been home too so they ordered a Chinese takeaway and slobbed about in their sweats and hoodies watching chick flicks until the early hours of the morning.

She thought about their chat. It'd been a tough one for her to bring up and an even harder one for Libby to discuss but it was needed, the air was crying out to be cleared.

"Lib, I've noticed things don't seem great with you and Jamie at the moment. What is going on?" She hadn't expected the reply she received so was shocked when the words came out.

"I knew this was coming I just didn't know when. No, things are not good and I am starting to wonder if they will ever get better."

Libby seemed calm. Like she had given it so much thought and had already made her mind up.

"What does that even mean? Have you guys ended or something? He is never here these days and you have literally not been over to his for weeks now. In fact, if it hadn't been for our night out then I'm not sure you would've seen him at all."

Libby looked at her hands. She seemed to be having an argument in her own head, despite trying to conceal her emotions, they were clear to see, written all over her face. If only she could read her thoughts she might be able to understand what was going on in there and be able to help.

"No, we are still together, at the moment. I have just realised a few things recently......especially after our argument....."

"I said all that in the heat of the moment, I didn't actually mean any of it. You guys are great together, you've come so far! C'mon ten years Libby, that is an awful lot to throw away."

"What if I have more to lose by staying with him?'
"I....I don't even know what that means?"

Libby had refused to talk any more about it and not long afterwards had made her excuses and gone to bed leaving Jane alone, her head throbbing from everything they'd just spoken about. She had then decided she should probably get some sleep as she had work the next day.

Once she was fully awake, she was annoyed to find her head still spinning, all she wanted to do was close her eyes and go back to sleep. About to do just that she suddenly remembered today was the day she was meeting Andrew. Sitting bolt upright as panic rose and her chest started pounding......*What the hell do I wear?*

When she walked into the kitchen an hour or so later she was shocked to see Libby up and about.

"Are you going into the office?" Jane casually asked her without looking up from the cupboard she was reaching inside for her favourite cereal.

"Yeah I will be leaving around 7am, there are a few things I need to catch up with after having yesterday off." Libby was staring at her, clearly waiting for last nights conversation to re-surface. She didn't have the energy, not this morning, not when she needed to clear her own head before 9am.

"So what time will you be in today?"

"Well I have an appointment at 9am so should be back after that. I haven't a clue how long it'll take though so can you keep looking through the database for a match for Dean? I have until 5pm before I have to give in and admit defeat."

"You're still meeting Andrew?"

"Yes, he's a paying client just like any other and the way things seem to be going lately we need all the extra business we can get. We don't do background checks on any of our other clients so they could all be serial cheaters for we know, we can't discriminate just because of a rumour."

"Are you sure it's a good idea though?"

"I won't believe it until I have heard it from his own lips. I mean the amount of kiss and tell stories there are floating around about him, they can't *all* be true can they?" Libby knew better than to push the conversation any further, and just like last night when she hadn't probed her for more information, Libby decided to return the favour.

~

She could feel her whole body shaking as she pulled outside Andrew's office building. She hadn't expected it to be quite as extravagant as this and seeing it towering above her made her feel she was totally out of her depth. Unsure where she was supposed to park she was relieved when a porter appeared at the side of the road and motioned to her.

Handing the keys over she stood and smoothed out her jacket. Having spent the best part of an hour sat in front of her wardrobe deliberating over what to wear, she'd eventually decided on a smart trouser suit with a hint of a pinstripe running through it. Wanting to remain professional but also not wanting to seem like a prude, she went for the suit that clung to her and highlighted each and every curve and womanly line her body had to offer. She wanted to be professional but she also wanted to make his mouth water when he looked at her and she knew there were ways of being sexy without flashing too much skin.

With their kiss still lingering in the forefront of her mind she became aware of how confused she was about this entire situation.Not knowing what to expect as she walked through the extravagant glass doors she braced herself. Even though she suspected it was going to be grand, she was still taken aback by the sheer size of the entrance. She realised she had no idea where she needed to go. By the looks of it he owned the whole bloody building.

Wishing she'd done her homework before coming she walked slowly over to the main reception desk. She was aware of the 'click clack' sound her high heels made as she made her way across the polished floor and wondered how she was supposed to act around him today especially when the last time they'd any face to face communication their tongues had been down each others throats. Exhaling deeply she found her voice and looked up at the pretty young girl who was smiling expectantly at her.

"Excuse me, I have a meeting with Mr Blake at 9am could you please tell me where I need to be?" She could hear the nerves reverberating in her voice and she hoped the woman hadn't noticed.

"Certainly, we have been expecting you Miss Aldrin. If you wait here someone will be down to escort you up." She gestured to the seating area to the left of her desk. It looked exactly like the departure lounge in an airport. Rows of low backed seats all joined together in a maze shape in order to utilise the space. She sat down, crossed her legs and exhaled loudly. She hadn't been aware she'd even been holding her breath.

Unsure what to do with herself she started counting the chairs, something she'd done from an early age to occupy her mind when she had nothing else to do. She'd made it to thirty before asking herself why anyone would need more than thirty seats in a waiting area? She was disrupted from her thoughts by a friendly face beaming down at her.

"Hello Miss Aldrin, I am Mr Blake's assistant, Rebecca. Would you like to follow me, he is ready for you."

She couldn't manage anything more than a nod and a smile. Silently she stood and followed her towards the lifts. *This is it.* She was about to see him.
Face to face after....

She felt hot under her suit just thinking about it and wanted to remove her jacket, but deciding against it she stepped into the lift. Not taking any notice of what floor they were heading to, just standing, finding it hard to breathe and incapable of speech. It seemed to take forever until she heard the familiar beeping sound which indicated they had reached their destination.

She followed Rebecca out the lift and towards a closed door. The walls were lined in walnut stained wood. It was so masculine and she wondered if he actually employed many women or if his business tailored to the needs of men alone. They passed a row of frosted glass windows and figured it must be some kind of boardroom, she wondered if he was waiting in there, but they continued walking. They were heading towards a closed door right at the end of the corridor. Rebecca paused at what must be her desk, situated just outside. She picked up her phone and waited. It didn't take long for her call to be answered.

"Mr Blake, Miss Aldrin is here to see you. Shall I bring her straight in?" She smiled and put the receiver down. Walking towards the closed door she had to stop and look back, Jane hadn't been able to follow.

"Miss Aldrin, Mr Blake is ready for you." Pushing open the door she had no choice now but to walk towards it and eventually she crossed the threshold into the huge airy room which was Andrew's office.

"Can I get you anything Mr Blake?" Rebecca seemed to be lingering, *she's just doing her job*, Jane told herself. Still, she wished she would hurry up and close the door so she could speak to him. That was if she could ever find her voice.

"No thank you, that will be all for now. Hold all my calls until further notice."

"Certainly sir."

He hadn't taken his eyes off Jane since the moment the door opened and even the distraction of Rebecca speaking made no difference to the connection his eyes had with her.

"Would you like to take a seat?" She looked in the direction his hand was pointing. There was a small round table positioned in the corner with two black leather chairs surrounding it. Little did she know it had been brought in especially for their meeting this morning.

She moved towards it with the intention of sitting down. Her legs feeling weak from the intensity of his stare, she wasn't sure how long she would be able to remain upright in these heels. He quickly moved in behind her to hold out the chair. She realised she would need to start talking and soon. She needed to find out what was going on, with them, with Ben's sister and with their work arrangement, but how to even begin?

"Can I get you a drink, coffee or tea?" She noticed a jug of water on the table and two crystal glasses, she motioned towards them.

"Water is fine, thank you." Her words came out weak and her voice strained. This was harder than she could ever have imagined. She watched him as he moved to the other side of the table and poured her drink. He placed an AB Inc coaster down before the now full glass and then seated himself on the remaining chair, his knees gently brushing hers as he positioned himself comfortably, all the while not breaking the connection to her with his eyes.

"Well I've been wondering where to start with all this. I have to say I've never been nervous about a meeting before, but after the last time I saw you......" She was thankful he'd pointed out the elephant in the room before she'd had to bring it up.

"I should apologise for Ben's actions the other night. He has these crazy ideas about you and....." She stopped, how did she tell this man he had supposedly screwed Ben's sister?

"I understand, it had nothing to do with you and nothing further will be done about it I assure you." He was so calm and composed, so why was it that she felt as if she was falling apart from the inside out? There was this undeniable chemistry between them that was so intense it literally took her breath away. Every time their knees touched under the small table it sent shock waves through her entire body. Swallowing hard, she tried to stay focussed.

"So, I guess we need to ascertain what to do with..... all this." Business, that was the best thing to figure out what was going on wasn't it? If he still wanted her services then he wasn't interested in *her*. Once they'd figured out the basis of their relationship, be it business or personal, then she would know how to move forward with this meeting.

"Jane we both know I want you. I am finding it hard not to jump on you right now after that kiss....." She felt her body tense. He was being so direct, it was unnerving. She hadn't expected any of this, and it had the strange effect of making her want him all the more.

She wanted to know exactly what he wanted to do to her. She wanted everything he had to offer. Licking her lips she was about to respond, but he jumped out of his seat distracting her from her thoughts. He was hard. At the mere sight of him straining inside his suit trousers she felt a tingle between her thighs. An urge to be satisfied washed over her like never before.

"I want you too..." Her voice came out raspy, she was losing all self control. All she wanted was him.

Without realising, she rose out her seat and began walking towards him. Unfazed by the fact that his office was 99% windows, she figured they were so high up no-one would be able to see anything anyway. She began removing her jacket revealing the small silky camisole underneath. There was a look in her eyes that told him she was about to devour him. He had his back to her but hearing her walking towards him made him spin around.

The sight of her seemed to shock him. She was now inches away from him, reaching her hand out she placed it on his shoulder before leaning in to trace her lips across his cheek. Enjoying the taste of him as she sought out his lips, not wanting to rush so took her time.

She felt Andrew tense at her touch. She knew this was crossing a line, but he made no movements to try and stop her so she continued. Finally locking her lips to his, starting off with tender kisses, savouring the time spent being so close to him, they quickly grew into a harder passionate embrace. She felt her entire world begin to shake.
She needed him.... now.
She needed him more than anything she'd ever needed before.

From this moment onwards He was her world and everything she did was for him. Moving her hands down, she teased off his tie and began unbuttoning his shirt, only stepping back to briefly admire his body. It was exactly as she'd expected, toned and tanned and simply delicious, but she needed to see more.

Before he let her unzip his pants, he slipped off her camisole revealing her ivory lace bra which did nothing to hide her erect nipples. He looked at both approvingly before reaching up to cup one, tweaking her nipple and gently rolling it between his finger and thumb making her groan loudly.

Jane's eyes had closed from the pleasure. She could feel his lips tenderly brushing her face, moving along her chin and down her neck before finally reaching the two mounds heaving intermittently to coincide with her rasps of pleasure.

He freed one of her breasts with a swift hand movement and Jane saw the hunger in his eyes. Feeling his mouth close around her nipple she lost what little control she had left. This had never felt so good, she could quite happily stay doing this for the rest of her life, although her nether regions were literally begging for some attention and it was too strong an urge to ignore much longer.

Opening her eyes during the briefest pause she stepped back, unzipped her trousers and shimmied out of them revealing a matching lace thong. Noticing him twitching, she knew it was his turn to be freed.

Without warning, as if he'd read her thoughts, he pulled off his trousers and boxers in one swift movement. She couldn't help but smile at what she saw. There was a lot of meat on offer and she was hungry.

Walking towards him she dropped to her knees. Wanting to taste every last inch of him, she took him into her mouth slowly and she carefully sucked and teased him until his legs began to shake beneath him. She could feel him struggling and her sex was screaming for its own release so she stood and guided him over to his desk chair.

Once he was seated she was about to resume her place on her knees but he stopped her. Hooking one finger into her panties he worked her clit as she hovered over him, her tits in his eye-line bouncing as her body reacted to his every touch. She wasn't sure she could take anymore when he thrust two fingers inside her. It was as if they were so in tune with one another no words were needed yet they both knew what the other wanted.

She was dripping wet but it seemed to make him want more. He became frantic in his actions and not even waiting to remove her pants just held them to one side as he guided her down on top of him.

"Oh god Jane!" He gasped as he entered her and she felt like she was about to explode around him then and there. It had *never* felt like this before. She relished every feeling as she pushed her hips lower wrapping her pussy entirely around him encasing him in her intimate warm embrace. She threw her arms around his head and twisted her fingers through his hair as she rocked back and forth in a feeling of sheer ecstasy.

She could feel her orgasm surfacing and knew she wouldn't last long, she wouldn't be able to hold it back. He was throbbing inside her and with every glide in and out they groaned loudly. Jane didn't care about the noise, she'd forgotten where they were and that Rebecca was sat right outside the door, she could probably hear each and every moan that escaped their lips, but right then it didn't matter…nothing mattered more than the two of them being together

Finally when neither of them could take anymore, the pressure having built to maximum capacity, they both boiled over the edge. Her body shuddered with the most phenomenal orgasm she'd ever experienced. Andrew held her firmly in place ready to take the full expanse of him as he throbbed and ejaculated deep inside her making her climax all over again.

They were wrapped in each others embrace, unmoving, catching their breath and enjoying the feeling of closeness before she decided now was the time to move and start re-dressing. Andrew silently stood did the same, his eyes now locked firmly to the floor. *Wow,* was the only thing running through her mind, all she wanted to do was jump around and dance, but didn't want to act childish in front of him. That could wait until she got back to the office. She knew they needed to discuss more than ever what was going on and what better time than right now. Things were definitely looking up after that and it was certainly something she wanted to do again.

"Well, that was ahh…" She couldn't think of the right words to use so stopped to bite on her bottom lip. She was thankful when he interrupted.

"Jane you are incredible, you really are." She felt like she was walking on air, if only he'd just stopped talking then.

"Jane….. that can never happen again. I am no good for you and I shouldn't have let that happen. I am sorry, I should've known better than to do any of….that." He started pacing his office, unable to look at her.

She was dumb struck.

She felt like she'd been hit by a truck.

He had completely shattered any good feelings she'd had and was now more confused than ever. How could he not have felt what she did? That was by far the best moment of her entire life and she'd been so sure that he felt the same. This didn't make any sense. She felt like the walls in the office were closing in on her, she couldn't breathe and desperately needed some air. She hadn't planned on this reaction and couldn't control the thoughts now rushing around her head.

"I……I don't…..I thought….I don't understand…"

"Jane, I employed you to find someone for me and that's exactly what I expect you to do. I am sorry for what just happened…… I understand if you feel you cannot work for me now but I know you're the best in what you do so I hope that's not the case." *He still wants me to find him someone!!! How can this be? This can't be happening!*

"Jane, *are* you still able to work for me and find me someone?" He asked a second time. She searched his eyes for any recognition that what had just happened had in fact meant anything to him, only to be disappointed to find it was like looking at a wall, not the vast and welcoming pool that had been there before.

He'd closed off to her, but why? Why was no good for her? All she knew was that she couldn't bear not to have him in her life. So, if this was the only way she could spend any time with him then it would have to do.

For now.

She made a promise that she would have him eventually.

"Yes." It was barely audible even to herself, so cleared her throat. Trying to formulate a plan in her head. she repeated.

"Yes." He seemed relieved and dropped back into the chair opposite her as if nothing out of the ordinary had happened between them.

CHAPTER 17

Hearing a knock, Libby looked up as Jamie's head appeared around the door.

"Didn't know if you fancied coming for lunch?" He scanned the room.

"She isn't back yet, she hasn't been in all morning. Wait, is it lunchtime already?" She'd been so engrossed in her work she hadn't noticed the time. *Where the hell is Jane?* She hadn't heard from her once since she'd left the flat that morning. Without thinking she picked up the phone and punched in Jane's mobile number.

"Damn it, voicemail." She began searching the computer address book for the number for Andrew's office, finding it she made a grab for the phone again.

"Libby what's the matter?" Jamie looked concerned.

"Jane had an appointment this morning with Andrew Blake, she still hasn't come back." There was a note of panic rising in her voice as she spoke. This wasn't like her. She'd been acting so out of character recently and Libby started to admit she was worried about her.
Ring ring, ring ring

"Come on....answer!"
Ring ring, ring ring

"Good afternoon AB Incorporated, Rebecca speaking how may I help you?"

"Oh hello this is Libby calling from Love Games, I was just looking for Jane, is she still there by any chance?"

"I'm sorry Miss Aldrin left an hour or so ago." *So where the hell is she then?* Libby knew you could get around London quickly if you had to, so it sure as hell wouldn't take an hour for her to get back to the office. Trying her mobile again she knew the only option she had was to leave a voicemail.

"Jane it's Lib, just checking in with you to make sure everything is alright. I'm popping out to lunch so call me as soon as you get this please…..I'm worried about you." Praying she would hear from her sooner rather than later, she put her phone on loud. She looked at Jamie, she'd only just remembered he was there.

"Where are we going then?"

It turns out not far, just to the little cafe round the corner. He didn't have long for lunch but felt he needed to see her, especially after the way things had been lately.

"Libby, I have been noticing some changes with us and I just wanted to make sure we were alright?" She was shocked. Jamie didn't talk about things like this, let alone talk about them out in public.

"I don't know what you mean, I have just been a bit busier than usual that's all." As the words toppled out her mouth she realised they were all lies. She knew now was the time to let him in. She had to tell him the truth. One thing she would never let herself become was a liar.

"Actually Jamie, that's not strictly true…..I have been working don't get me wrong, but it's nothing to do with Jane. In fact she has no idea what I have been doing either before you start on her."

"What are you going on about?" *How am I going to start explaining all this? Best to just be honest and start from the beginning,* she thought quickly.

"Well I've never given up on my dream to be a fashion designer and I never intend to." The look on his face told her she hadn't made the best start. Starting off on the defensive was never a good choice.

"But you haven't done anything for years!"

"Not that you know about, no. I've been working on my current portfolio in secret and have been using most of my money to have my designs made up into garments ready for the day I can pitch my work to some companies."

"But why are you telling me this now? Have you got another job or something?"

"No! Not yet but things are looking up what with Ben being a model.." He cut her off mid sentence,

"Wait, Ben? The lunatic who attacks people when their backs are turned?" Okay, so he was pissed off, his voice was rising and she didn't want to draw attention to them. People were starting to notice and were looking over. She needed to calm him down.

"Sshh, yes Ben the one whose sister was hurt by the man he attacked. The one who thought that same man had done something to our friend Jane, remember her??"

"Well he can't have scared her that much if she still ran off to meet the guy today."

"Look this isn't about Jane, this is about me for a change!" Now it was her turn to get angry. She narrowed her eyes and folded her arms. It looked like now was going to be the time to be honest about her feelings.

"What's that supposed to mean?"

"You don't seem to realise how much I have to turn a blind eye to being with you. I seemingly gave up on my one dream and you didn't bat an eyelid, you didn't encourage me to keep going with it, you just thought oh well you have an income be satisfied. BE SATISFIED? Well you know what I AM NOT SATISFIED!" She threw her napkin down onto the table and marched out onto the street. Jamie quickly followed her, ignoring the sideways glances and sniggers from the tables around them.

"Why didn't you tell me any of this?" He grabbed her wrist to stop her from walking away from him.

"Libby, for fucks sake, talk to me. Don't you see this is why we are in this mess because YOU never talk to ME about these things!" Turning on him she felt all the emotions she'd been trying to ignore come bubbling to the surface until she could hold them back no longer. *He* was blaming *her* for all this!

"ME?! How dare you blame me for this. YOU are the one that puts no effort into US. YOU are the one that stays away cause you don't seem to like being around Jane anymore. YOU are the one that has stifled any dreams I've ever had and made me stay trapped in this life where I can never. Get. Anywhere! Meeting Ben was like a breath of fresh air and HE is helping me. HE believes in me. Something I should've expected from the man I gave ten years of my fucking life to!"

"I…..I had no idea……Libby I thought you were happy…. If I knew….."

"You have always known my dreams Jamie, you just never did anything about them…….I just don't think we are meant to be anymore." That was it, she'd said it out loud.

"Libby think about this before you say anything you might regret."

"Regret! Oh I won't regret it believe me. The only regrets I have are that I wasted the best part of my life settling for what everyone else thought was good for me… We want different things out of life……. I think it's best we call it a day." She couldn't believe she'd actually said the words she had been frightened to admit for so long. Jamie looked dumbstruck. His face had fallen and he looked sadder than she'd ever seen him before.

She looked away before the sight of him reduced her to tears, or she changed her mind about the whole thing. There were people all around them, couples hand in hand smiling at each other as they looked in shops and chatted away without a care in the world. Elderly and young, men and women all getting on with their day to day lives blissfully unaware of the heartbreak occurring right next to them.

"Libby, please…." He couldn't finish his sentence. What was he going to ask for, another chance? Even if she gave him one she knew nothing would change, then what would happen if she had to move to Paris? She knew full well he would hate her going out there on her own, but would hate it even more if she dragged him along with her. No, this had to be the best option for both of them.

She did love him, you can't be with someone for as long as they had and not feel anything anymore. It had just gotten more like a brother sister relationship and the complete lack of intimacy had re-enforced that even more. She liked his company and felt comfortable around him, but she needed someone who was going to support her, challenge her, and keep her on the right track. She knew, deep down, this wasn't something he was capable of doing.

"I'm so sorry…… it's over. I have to focus on getting what I want now. That might seem totally selfish to you, but if I don't do it now I never will and I don't want to live my life with any more regrets and blame you for them. I'm….I'm so sorry." Fighting back tears, she pecked his cheek and walked away, making sure she didn't turn back and have one last look at him, knowing it would break her heart to see him standing there. Alone. But this had to be done, she had to make a fresh start. And it had to be without him.

CHAPTER 18

Andrew slammed down his phone. He was angry, so much so he couldn't help but take it out on everyone around him. That one ridiculous moment of weakness, letting himself have exactly what he wanted could have cost him everything. He knew what people said about him and there he was letting himself get fucked in his office by someone he barely knew.

What if she runs off to the papers and told them everything? Even as the thought crossed his mind he knew she wasn't like that. Why couldn't he let himself see where things could go with her? He felt a connection with her and couldn't imagine not having her in his life, so why had he been so adamant that she find someone else for him?

He couldn't think straight to answer any of his questions and that was making him all the more infuriated. Since Carol, he hadn't felt this way about anyone but knew he couldn't let her get close. The only thing he was sure about was that he was bad for her and he didn't want to be the one that broke her heart.

"Rebecca get me a coffee." He barked through the intercom. There was no response but moments later she walked into his office with a steaming pot of fresh coffee.

"Here you are sir. So…how did it go?" She motioned towards the round table that still had bits of paperwork strewn on it which Jane had left for him. Pricing plans and a copy of the profile they'd set up together after…well after IT happened. He couldn't bear to look at it.

"Fan-fucking-tastic!" She looked astonished, he'd never spoken out of turn before. She'd gotten under his skin and he was losing all resolve. He needed to get Rebecca out. No-one should see him like this.

"Sir, is everything alright? Miss Aldrin left quickly after…… did…did something happen?" He looked up into her face to study her eyes. *Surely not,* he thought. *I always thought you of all people would believe I am not THAT guy!*

"What's that supposed to mean?" He looked dishevelled and not his usual pristine self. Certainly not the Andrew Blake, successful business man who strode into the office that morning.

"I just meant...."

"Oh I know what you meant, just get out!! And Rebecca, if that's what you think then...don't come back." What was he doing? He felt so out of control he just couldn't stop himself.

"What? You don't mean? Surely not!" The look he gave was enough clarification and she marched out of his office only pausing to collect her things on the way.

He was cursing. How could he have just spoken to her like that? With his head in his hands he knew he had some serious grovelling ahead of him in order to get her back.
He needed her.
She was the only person in his life he could be honest with and knew would speak the truth to him.

How could Jane have gotten to him like this? He knew just one thing, it was in her best interests to stay well away from him. He hurt the people he loved and he would not have her be his next victim. He hoped if he told himself often enough he'd eventually start believing it.

CHAPTER 19

Jane's alarm went off at 6.30am. She'd managed to get through the rest of the day without breaking down or confessing what had happened to Libby, both in Andrew's office and after, knowing that going to see William would start yet another row, but he'd been the first person she thought of who could help her forget everything.

Sure she was angry with him but she went to him knowing she wasn't going to let anything happen. She used her expert flirting techniques to make him want her, and it was just the ego boost she needed. After what had happened with Andrew, she needed to feel wanted and she didn't care who it was doing the wanting.

Sitting up on the side of her bed she pulled her Filofax out her handbag, absentmindedly flicking to the notes she'd made for today. Starting the day knowing exactly what was happening and when made her feel like she had some control of her life especially when it felt like things were spiralling out of her jurisdiction.

It was the usual crap, couple of phone appointments, more searching for Dean's perfect match, something she'd started to believe she had no chance of succeeding with. She was going to have to admit defeat and offer the poor bloke a refund. Then a note that hadn't been written by her caught her attention.

8pm - Neil.

Who wrote this, and when for that matter? It didn't take long before it dawned on her that this was Joanna's handiwork. But how had she managed to get it in her diary without her knowing?

***

8pm on the dot and the flats intercom system started buzzing. Both girls screamed with excitement making Libby spill wine all over herself. Libby hadn't broken down once since revealing that her and Jamie had split and Jane knew it was only a matter of time before some emotion crept out. Still, while she was remaining strong things could carry on as normal and she would be there for her as and when she needed her.

She hadn't heard from anyone about what was happening tonight so hadn't been sure whether to get ready for a date or not. Walking to the phone to answer it she realised how awkward she felt. It might not even be him and then how foolish would she look. At least she could blame Libby, it was her that'd talked her into getting ready for this weird date. She'd gone on about how it could be her fairytale ending, especially with all the mystery and intrigue.

"Hello?"

"It's Neil I hope I'm not late."

"No, right on time." She smiled. He hadn't stood her up at least.

"Do you want to come up?" She'd planned to get him inside the flat, that way she could gauge what he was wearing to see if she needed to change before they left.

"Yes that would be nice, thank you." She buzzed him through the main door and waited to let him in when he made it up the stairs.

"Hello again." He leant in to kiss both her cheeks. *Very Hollywood,* she thought, actually it was very Joanna. She shivered at the thought and hoped this was where their similarities ended.

This was how she felt she deserved to be treated, not used like the last few men she'd been involved with. Thoughts of Andrew and William came rushing back and she faltered. Negative thoughts and contradictions rooted her to the spot and she felt the need to run to her room, lock it and never venture back out.

No Jane, remember what you said, your new mission is to be so busy loving life that you have no time for hate, regret, worry or fear, starting from tonight! Giving herself a good talking to as Libby introduced herself to him.

"Do you want a drink while I finish getting ready?"

"No I am fine thank you. You look lovely as you are though. You needn't change."

"I am a tad overdressed." She blushed, she'd taken in his appearance as soon as he walked in. Firstly she had been relieved he wasn't sporting one of his over-sized suits, but she was a bit surprised to find that he was wearing jeans. He hadn't opted for trainers but had some tan suede slip on shoes that were the next best thing to a trainer in her opinion. His jacket was a shade lighter than his shoes but it looked to be made of the same material. She couldn't make out what was underneath but whatever it was looked plain and black and not the sort of thing you would expect on a first date.

Feeling silly in the little green dress she'd chosen to wear, she made her way back into her room, pulling on her favourite pair of skinny jeans and a tight knitted top before finishing the look off with her favourite blazer and some low heeled ankle boots. She felt much better but wondered what they could be doing dressed like this, Jane was eager to find out.

"Right, I'm ready now. What are we doing exactly?"

"All in good time." And with that he offered her his arm and escorted her towards the front door. Looking back she got a nod of approval from Libby who had slumped herself on the sofa and was in the process of pouring yet another glass of wine. Jane wondered if the approval was for her quickly thrown together outfit or Neil. She would have to try and find out later.

He didn't have a flash car. It was just a box standard Volvo in a silvery grey colour but it was nice enough and made a welcome break from having to take the tube at this time of night. She saw they were getting close to Euston Station, she began to wonder if perhaps he was taking her out of London entirely. She'd started to daydream about hopping on a train and leaving all her troubles in London behind. The more she thought about it the more it seemed like a great idea.

He made a swift turn and eventually parked up at the entrance to London Zoo.

"Oh I haven't been here since I was little!!" She couldn't contain her excitement, she was fidgeting around in her seat and Neil was grinning at her from the drivers seat. *Someone has done their homework,* she mused.

"But I thought the park closed at like 6pm?" She was looking around for the noticeboard with the opening times on, the whole place was in darkness and seemingly deserted.

"I pulled a few strings, we have a couple of hours then I have a table reserved in a place nearby if you will have some dinner with me?"

"This is amazing, how did you…..?" But she didn't need to know the answer. The fact that he'd gone to so much effort for her made her want to keep the mystery. No-one had ever gone to this much trouble for a first date, not with her anyway. *Maybe Libby is right about my happy ending,* she thought.

She'd loved going to the zoo when she was a child. It had been the place her and Libby's parents took them to let off some steam and go crazy running around the vast expanse of space and enclosures. Adulthood didn't allow time for places such as the zoo, so it had been a long time since she'd last been there.

She was aware that a lot of people hated zoo's and thought it cruel to keep animals so far away from their natural habitat, stuck in cages with only limited amounts of space in which to occupy themselves. Despite that, she felt that zoo's were magical places which let you see the amazing things the world had to offer without having to actually travel the globe to see them.

Giraffe's, lions and gorilla's had always been her favourites. She could just about remember where their enclosures were. She was wondering how things might have changed since she'd last been. So much so she hadn't realised she'd slid out the car and had started walking towards the gates. He slipped out and followed her. He was grinning.

"Now, I know you like lions, but they are in the process of building a new enclosure so there isn't a lion display at the moment."

"Oh that's a shame. We still have gorilla's and giraffe's though. Come on, we don't have long and I want to make the most of the time we do have." She grabbed his hand and tugged him through the entrance, both giggling like a pair of teenagers doing something they shouldn't.

~

The couple of hours at the zoo went by like a dream. She'd watched the animals in awe like she'd used to when she was younger and Neil had captivated her attention whilst making her feel perfectly at ease. He knew a lot about her already, courtesy of Joanna, so she used their time to find out more about him.

He was only a couple of years older than her, although he seemed around the same age as Andrew from his mannerisms and the way he acted around her. The phrase an old head on young shoulders kept springing to mind. He'd moved to London when he was in his twenties to try and forge a career in journalism. Having freelanced for a few years, he eventually landed a job in Joanna's office working for the local paper. To date he'd had several front page stories and was proud of each and every one of them. The way he had gone on about them was as if he'd changed the world just with his words alone. His work obviously meant a lot to him.

The time had flown by and they were soon being ushered out of the park. As soon as she was inside the car her stomach growled loudly. She'd been so busy enjoying herself she hadn't realised how hungry she was. She hadn't been able to hide it and felt her face flush at the embarrassment of the giveaway sound.

"Come on, lets get you fed." He nodded towards her stomach and switched the engine on. He drove them to a little public house not too far from Euston Station. It was a quaint looking building, it wasn't very large but looked good and seemed to be busy.

Walking in, Jane was gob-smacked. This was like nothing she'd ever experienced in London before. It looked more like a countryside pub than something in a big city like London. Dark beams visible overhead and log fires burning in almost every corner. The food smelt divine, making her stomach cry out again.

She was desperate to eat so when Neil walked her over to a table she grabbed some menu's along the way. It wasn't the most extensive menu she'd ever seen, but looking around she noticed they served decent sized portions. Everything from traditional roasts to home-made pies, it all sounded amazing.

"Oh this all sounds lush. I have no idea what to go for."

"I have it on good authority that the fish and chips are exceptional here." He winked at her.

"I take it you come her quite a lot then?"

"I have been known to dine here every now and then, yes."

"Well I will take your word for it. Do you want to go and order or shall I?"

"I'll go, you sit and relax."

Having decided on the beer battered fish, chunky chips and minted pea option, she sat back and for the first time in a long time, relaxed. Closing her eyes she basked in the warmth of the pub, taking in the varying scents of food as dish after dish were brought out to the tables around her. Listening to the gentle chitter chatter of all the happy people surrounding her meant she didn't hear Neil come back or that he was trying to talk to her.

"Oh sorry, I was just taking all this in. It's...it's amazing." Once again she could feel the blush spread across her face. This was becoming a regular occurrence over the past few days and she didn't like it.

"That's ok. I just asked how it is that an amazingly attractive and talented lady such as yourself hasn't gotten herself a husband yet? You've had so many successful matches in your business, why haven't you made one for yourself?" *Oh!* Jane hadn't been asked this question before, especially not on a date, they usually left her line of work at the door for fear that she was going to use some of her techniques to get them to fall madly in love with her and propose marriage there and then. She was a good match maker, she wasn't however a miracle worker and sadly did not possess those kinds of powers.

"I pick the wrong men. It really is as simple as that." Admitting it out loud she knew that was the sole basis of her single status.

"But how can you be so successful in match making when you aren't for yourself?"

"I guess I can't be that good." She let out a giggle but she was concerned that if he thought this, then other people would too.

"I do worry that people will take one look at my dating history and think erm no you aren't qualified to find someone for me. You can't even date a guy for very long let alone settle down with anyone. You have no idea what love is." She laughed again but something she'd said seemed to pique his interest further.

"But surely you've felt love before?" He was looking at her intently, his eyes bored into hers almost as if he were trying to see into the depths of her soul. She shifted uncomfortably in her seat.

"I think I may have, but I am probably wrong." She was forced to think about Andrew. Could what she felt for him be love? She'd never felt it before so how would she know if she'd fallen?

Love was such a scary word, one that most people avoided saying until they were sure about it, while others banded it around so often that it no longer had any meaning. Surely people knew when they had fallen in love didn't they? You heard it all the time, people saying *'oh I knew right away he was the one for me,'* but then Libby had said this about Jamie and now look at them. *Can you really just know?* Her mind was working on overload, she wasn't concentrating on anything he was saying to her, just trying to figure out what her own feelings were.

"So what do you really think of love, is it all it's cracked up to be or just a waste of time?"

Love.....what do I think of love?

"Honestly, until recently I didn't think love was real. I thought it was just something people wanted and then settled for the best they could get. I knew it was something I could capitalise on and use to make some money from." Until she said it aloud she hadn't realised how harsh her words sounded. She was using people's loneliness as a means to make money. It was harsh but true. She was living off people's insecurities and inability to find love.

"Until recently? What's happened to make you change your mind?" She didn't have chance to answer as they were interrupted by their food coming out. Quickly taking a bite of her chips she groaned loudly, forgetting everything they'd just been speaking about.

"Mmmm, this is sooo good!" With that, their talk of love and business seemed to have disappeared.

CHAPTER 20

"Do you know what, I give up. Dean must be looking for a woman that simply doesn't exist, hey should we try him with some men, maybe he doesn't know he has turned?" Libby called over to her.

Jane laughed, there was always the possibility that they were having so much trouble setting him up because he was in-fact looking at the wrong gender entirely. Not that this was something she could suggest to him, she'd already embarrassed him enough with the crappy date she'd sent him on, there was no chance she was doing it again.

She was in the best mood she'd been in for a while and with the date last night still fresh in her mind she had lots to smile about, despite having an awkward client to try and sort out. Opening her folder to check out the state of her to-do-list, her good mood faltered. Right at the top was the unbearable task of setting Andrew up with his 'perfect' woman.

Secretly praying she'd have the same troubles with him as she was having with Dean she pulled up the female database on her computer. After punching in some of the key details taken from his profile, she began trawling through the list of possible suitors her fancy programme pulled up for her. Deleting one after another, she began to smile. *Maybe he is like Dean after all, too picky for his own good,* she thought when her eyes were suddenly drawn to one profile.

Caroline Evans.

On paper she looked near on perfect for him. Moving over to the filing cabinet she searched for the full file. Slipping it out the drawer she returned to her desk flipping it open eager to read more about the woman who seemed so perfect for the man she couldn't get out of her head.
Same age. Tick.
Divorced. Tick, well at least they could swap stories if they didn't have anything else to talk about.
No children. Tick.

Jeez they even have the same interests. Literature, movies, theatre, fine dining, it was like she was made just for him. *Looks like she has just landed herself her first publication too so she should be right up his street being an author,* Jane thought, remembering the extensive array of books he'd had in his office.

Caroline had been happy to be held on file until her best match came along, unlike Dean and Andrew who'd paid the premium for active searching.

"Bloody hell I think I have found someone for Andrew, can you believe that?" She hadn't recounted exactly what had happened at his office and had made sure her make-up was pristine again before returning, so there was no evidence left of the tears she'd shed. Libby had no idea about any of it.

"Well that didn't take long did it? What five minutes or so? See you've still got it babe."

"Well she has been on the books for a long time, I'll be lucky if she hasn't found someone all by herself."

"Call her, oh right, you have to run it by him first don't you. Call him.. call him now!"

"Ok, calm down, I'll call him when you are out on lunch so I can have a bit of privacy. I still need to do the compatibility questionnaires and all the other paperwork before I do anything. Have I taught you nothing?" Rolling her eyes she knew she'd gotten away with having to speak to him while Libby was there. She wasn't sure how she was going to remain composed on her own, but having to do it in front of her would be even worse and was sure to raise unwanted questions. Ones she wasn't sure was able to answer right now.

"Speaking of lunch, I am out of here in 5 ok?"

"Is it that time already? Hey, wanna grab me a sandwich and a coffee while you are out? Take an hour and a half to give me enough time to make this call ok?"

"You don't have to tell me twice!" With that Libby hopped out the office.

Jane completed the necessary paperwork and, it was just as expected, they were so alike they must have meant to be together. Realising she was going to have to make the call she clammed up. The sound of his voice alone would bring back so many emotions she'd tried hard to suppress.

Inhaling deeply she picked up the phone and punched in the number she'd jotted down on her pad earlier, when the thought that he might not even be there flashed into her head she allowed herself to relax. She regretted it as soon as the call was answered.

"Good afternoon AB Incorporated, Rebecca speaking how may I help you?"

"Oh hello, this is Jane Aldrin calling from Love Games, I wondered if Mr Blake was available?"

"I will just check for you." Hearing a beep and then silence, she knew she'd been put on hold. She made a mental note to tell him he needed to invest in hold music. How he'd spent a small fortune for his waiting area yet hadn't invested in hold music was beyond her.
Click

"Jane….how are you?" She'd been expecting to hear Rebecca's voice so was stunned when *his* voice appeared on the other end.

"Hi, I'm, yeah, I'm fine thank you, how are you?"

"Are you sure you're alright? I'm surprised to be hearing from you so soon after…..our meeting."

"Yes I am fine, why wouldn't I be? It's about our meeting I'm calling actually." There was nothing but silence at the other end of the phone. It distracted her thoughts but she carried on, the sooner she made her match the sooner she could get him out of her life and more importantly, out of her head.

"Well it's good news, we have found you a match and I wanted to know if you wanted me to make the initial set up for you?"

"Oh, I wasn't expecting that. A match…already?" *What was he expecting? Was he waiting for me to declare my undying love for him or say I can no longer work for him because my own feelings are getting in the way?* The truth was she did want to be with him. Why was she feeling this way? It was so stupid, he'd told her it wasn't going to happen. She didn't like feeling out of control, especially when it came to her emotions.

"Well I am just doing my job like you asked me to do. Nothing more, nothing less." *There, that should answer any questions*, she thought arrogantly.

"Yes, yes I suppose I did didn't I? Then yes, please do the necessary set up, email me the details." His voice had turned cold. Jane wondered why he'd closed off to her all of a sudden but knew it would be inappropriate to ask.

"Certainly. Her name is Caroline Evans but I won't divulge any further information so you have plenty to talk about during your first date."

"Thank you….. Jane." The pause made her think he wanted to say more but couldn't find the words. She would probably never find out as she was so sure this match would be the one for him she even considered getting a hat in ready for when the wedding invitation came through.Hanging up she felt deflated and wondered if he felt the same intensity whenever he spoke to her or if it was all just in her head. Had she once again fallen for the wrong guy?

Picking the phone back up she found Caroline's number. As she was dialling she was thinking how lucky this woman was about to be.

"Hello?"

"Hello is this Caroline Evans?"

"Speaking."

"Oh hello, my name is Jane I'm calling from Love Games dating agency, are you able to talk for a few moments?

"Oh, yes of course."

"Well as you know you requested your file to be held on our system until a suitable match was found and I am calling today to tell you we have now made a 99% match. Would you be happy to go on a date with him?"

"Oh my. Well it's been a little while so I 'm not sure how I feel about it all now." She was giggling so Jane knew this was just bravado. She was desperate to go on this date, she just didn't want to show exactly how desperate she was.

"It's just an initial meeting and if you like him we go from there, if you don't, you go back on our files until another match is made for you."

"99% hey? Ok, then yes why not. You only live once don't you?" There was that giggle again. The sound seemed to reverberate through her. She had never met this woman and for all she knew she could be the next best thing to Mother Teresa, but there was one thing she was sure of….she absolutely despised her.

Jane set about arranging their date and emailed the details to them both once she'd finalised it all. She sat back wishing it was her that was getting the date with Andrew and not the vile giggly woman. She decided to kill a bit of time and fill out a compatibility questionnaire for herself, just to see what percentage she got. She knew it would be no-where near the 99% Caroline got, but she was so intrigued she couldn't stop herself.

Hearing a knock on the door she looked up, she wasn't expecting anyone and was surprised when no-one came through. She stood to open it and was left face to face with William. Instantly wishing she'd stayed where she was and left him thinking no-one was there.

"Jane baby, where have you been hiding?" He drawled at her. He had a look in his eye like he was hungry and she was about to be his main course.

"William! What are you doing here?" She scrunched up her face, confusion written all over it.

"I came to see you. You show up at my office the other day, flirt the crap out of me knowing full well I can't touch, then I don't hear from you again, what's up with that?" He walked into the room even though

Jane hadn't made a space for him to pass, forcing him to brush up against her. He came across so masterful, shame he was a complete jerk.

"I have been busy. But i'm sure you haven't been short of other offers, you never used to be!" Everyone knew about his reputation so it was pointless him trying to deny it.

"Ouch, Jane, that cut deep! It's not just me playing the field is it though? Everyone knows about your date with Nerdy Neil last night."

"Wait, what?"

"You mean you don't know? Oh this is gold. Why don't you call your little assistant up and get her to grab you a copy of today's paper on her way back in. In the meantime...." He walked towards her ignoring the questioning look that now had her eyebrows knotted together.

He began kissing her neck and groping her breasts. She felt...... nothing. It was as if the spell he once had over her had been lifted. Well either lifted or just shifted on to someone else.

William had always appeared dominant and experienced, but today he seemed, clumsy. He certainly wasn't getting her going the way he used to. All she could think about was what he'd just said and she wanted to know what he'd meant.

Pushing him away from her at the exact moment Libby chose to walk back into the office. She screeched as she saw them pull apart.

"What. The. Fuck?" William was comically trying to conceal his raging hard on and Jane was shifting around, still trying to work out what he had been talking about.

"Libby, it's not what it looks like ok." She started but Libby interjected instantly.

"Look, I don't really care anymore, you are a big girl and can make as many mistakes as you like but YOU..." She rounded on William.

"You need to leave, NOW!" There was a sense of desperation in her tone that made her feel uneasy.

"Libby, what's happened?"

"Not now, get rid of *him* first." She looked at William who seemed to be enjoying all the drama and was making no effort to even try and disappear.

"I think you should probably go." Nodding towards the door to make sure he fully understood. He let out an exasperated sigh and started moving towards it. Turning back, he looked her up and down and left his parting comment.

"I've no doubt I will be seeing you later!" With that he slipped on his Aviator sunglasses and closed the door behind him with a sharp flick.

"Jane there is no easy way to say this.... you...... you just need to see this." Libby thrust a copy of a newspaper into her hands and was visibly shaking as she handed it over.

"Turn to page 6..." Libby closed her eyes as she opened it and let out a sharp gasp. She looked down and saw a huge image of her face staring back up at her.

"What...what is this?" Libby didn't reply, just stood there as Jane's eyes scanned the paper. The headline read;

Love Lies, The true feelings of Love Games Director Jane Aldrin.

Catching the small print she noted it had been written by none other than Neil Moore. Neil! *Was this what William had been on about?* She read though the article, then read it again and again until all the words on the page blurred into one big blob due to the uncontrollable well of tears that'd filled her eyes and were now overspilling onto the page. This article was going to finish her business off for sure. Who in their right mind was going to come to her for help finding love when it was here in black and white how she really felt about it? The answer... no-one. She was finished!

"Look, people don't always believe what they read in the papers hun." It was as if Libby had read her mind. She felt numb and couldn't find any words to respond, she couldn't tear her eyes away from the article long enough to formulate a sentence. How could he have done this to her? They'd had such a lovely date and she genuinely wanted to see him again, she couldn't get her head round this blatant deceit. He'd gone to so much effort to please her and it had all been for...this! This story!

"Jane, you are worrying me now, please speak to me." But at that same moment the phone rang and she had no choice but to answer it.

"Erm, Jane.....it's Joanna... I can tell her it's not convenient if you don't want to speak to her."

Hearing the name snapped Jane back into the present. Joanna!! Did she know about this? Was she in on it?

Without speaking and not letting go of the article gripped tightly in her hands, she rushed to the phone. Snatching it out of Libby's hands before she lost her courage.

"You had better not be behind this Joanna, I swear to god you will regret it if you are....."

"Jane, I am truly sorry. Yes, I knew Neil wanted a story out of you which is why he was so persistent about going on a date.... But it wasn't supposed to be like this." She could hear the remorse in her voice but didn't buy it. From anyone else maybe, but Joanna was a law unto herself.

"What *was* it supposed to be then?" She bit back only just getting the words out as she clenched her jaw, gritting her teeth as if she was afraid what might come out if she didn't.

"He was supposed to do a positive article. Promoting your business. Helping you out a little. Your mother thought you could do with a boost, keep things ticking over for you, she mentioned something maybe going in the paper and I helped set it up. I had no idea this is what would happen I assure you."

Well it was one thing that Joanna wasn't behind the dish the dirt story, but the fact that her own mother had thought she needed help, and what was with all the secrecy and going behind her back. Her own mother of all people should know that she hated people being underhand and deceitful. She felt utterly humiliated.

She could no longer speak, simply dropped the receiver and walked over to her desk. Staring at the words glaring menacingly back up at her, *'Love is something I could capitalise on and use to make money from'*. These were *her* words so why did they look so alien?

Her thoughts flashed to Andrew, as they often did these days. Had he seen this? What would he think of her? She would probably lose all her clients which was going to hurt like hell, but if she lost him, well that would hurt more than any of it. She couldn't hold back the fresh wave of tears, they filled her eyes making her momentarily blind before spilling over and pouring down her cheeks. It was like the banks had broken and she couldn't stop the endless flow. Now she'd started there was no stopping.

Libby picked up the phone and finished the call for her. Hanging up, she sat at her desk not knowing what to do or how to help. The computer was going mad, email after email filtering through. Jane noticed them too and was about to begin opening them.

"Jane, you don't need to do this now. Why not leave these to me and go home?" She knew the emails were going to be from clients withdrawing themselves from her books. She knew the article would have had a serious effect on her business but she needed to see just how bad it was.

"No, no I need to do this." Biting her lip she went to the first unread message and clicked it open.

After what I have read today I no longer wish you to represent me. Please remove me immediately and do not contact me again.

Well it was expected and it could have been a whole lot worse. After reading through several more Jane found most people had opted to keep their messages short and to the point. There were, of course, the odd few that really went to town with their abuse and those were the ones that brought about a fresh waves of tears each time.

Sixty seven emails later and she was almost done with the back log. She felt drained and hopeless. How the hell was she going to bounce back from this? Hearing Libby's mobile ringing, she took the opportunity to go and make coffee to give her friend some privacy. The noise of the kettle drowned out Libby's chatter but she could just make out a hint of glee that was quickly hushed to a more muted level.

Her brain was empty, she was numb. She couldn't even function to prepare her coffee and was still standing there unmoving when the kettle clicked off again.

"I really think you should go home." Jane couldn't be sure how long she'd been standing there, but the way Libby was watching her indicated it had been longer than was deemed socially acceptable.

Her shoulders were shaking and she knew she couldn't stay strong any longer. Feeling Libby's arms embrace her, she rested her head on her shoulder and cried. She cried like she'd never cried before. She thought she was never going to be able to stop. She felt she might just keep on crying like this for the rest of her life and began to wonder if it was possible for your tear ducts to actually run dry.

When Libby released her she slid down to the floor. Having lost the last ounce of energy she had left, she was weak and now she was having trouble breathing.

Her chest felt tight.

Her breath was coming out in short, sharp rasps.

She wanted to curl up as small as she could make herself and hide there until the pain went away, never having to face anyone ever again.

Libby was forced away by the phones ringing off the hook, knowing it would be more unhappy people cancelling their contracts and asking for refunds. Jane began sobbing until she eventually closed her eyes and drifted off to sleep right there on the tiny space on the floor.

CHAPTER 21

Jane was surprised to find herself at home on her sofa when she regained consciousness. How she'd gotten there she had absolutely no idea, but her head was curled up against Libby who was holding her hand and softly stroking it. She heard other voices but couldn't make out who they were coming from. It wasn't until she was fully awake that she heard her mother and father busying themselves in the kitchen. They were having a heated discussion about something, but she felt too weak to try and listen in. She was pretty sure Joanna would be at the root of it somehow.

"Hey, Jane you're awake. Do you want coffee?" Libby was talking to her like she was a child. Great, so she had to lose her dignity as well as her whole fucking life because of one stupid ball-bag.

"Coffee, thanks." She sat herself up. Her whole body ached, she felt like she'd been hit by a bus. She couldn't remember what'd happened to make her feel this bad.

Libby slumped off to the kitchen, but her seat wasn't left empty for long, being quickly replaced by her mother who shuffled in close and threw her arms around her. Squeezing out what little life she had left.

"I wish Id've known. Joanna said it would help the business, not close it down. Darling I am so sorry. If I hadn't mentioned it to her...." She watched as her mother brushed away a tear and stifled a sob.

"It's not finished yet Mum, I will fight this." Her mum glanced nervously at her dad before looking back at her and answering.

"Of course dear, of course."

"Wait...Has something else happened? Libby, how many people have been in touch?"

"Not now dear, just try and relax this afternoon. Joanna is on the case at the paper trying to get a retraction printed, but it's not looking so good at the moment. Apparently Neil is getting inundated with offers of stories about you and the company and it's believed they will be good for the paper." She wanted to smile at the look of disgust on her mothers face as she said Neil's name out loud, but was too exhausted to translate the emotion to her face.

"How did I get here though? I was in the office....the coffee..."

"You had a panic attack love. Libby found you on the floor and called me and your dad to bring you home right away. Well we were so worried about you my darling!" If she wasn't so emotionless she might have found the whole scenario quite funny, but the more she thought about it she didn't think she would have anything to laugh about ever again.

"I still have some clients don't I?" Aiming this question at Libby as she brought the coffee over.

"Yyyes." She stammered, "we still have *some* people on the books. But Jane, if there are going to be further stories I'm worried that you won't be able to pull anything back from this." Her parents shot Libby a stern look but she pleaded her case.

"Well??? She has to know the truth doesn't she, what is the point in lying to her and getting her hopes up? Best she knows everything, ALL cards on the table!"

"Well if we are being honest then you had better tell her *your* news!" Jane's Mum spat back.

"What's that supposed to mean? Hey, will someone tell me what the hell is going on?"

"Jane!" Her dad reprimanded her. He could sense an argument brewing and tried to dissipate it before it really got going. Her dad was a man of very few words, he much preferred to sit back and observe, and lets face it, her mother did so much talking he'd probably gotten used to her saying it all for the two of them by now.

"Jane, Libby had some news today and she wasn't going to say anything just yet but it seems your mother now thinks you should know." His tone told her he was annoyed, her Mum had played dirty at her expense. She didn't care, she just wanted to know what was happening so turned to Libby who was looking at the floor in-front of her as if her life depended on it.

"Libby?"

Silence....

"LIBBY? I swear to God if you don't tell me the shit is gonna hit the fan."

"I...ahh...I..I have to go to Paris tomorrow."

"Paris? Why?"

"I sort of have some interviews out there."

"Work? What? I don't understand! Why Paris?"

"I've been working on a new portfolio and Ben helped set some up meetings for me to hopefully start my career in fashion. I have been meaning to tell you but there's never been the right moment."

"Ben? Ben, Ben? THE Ben who I introduced you to?"

"Yes…"

"When did you plan this? Why did you go behind my back?" Jane felt a betrayal like never before.

"I am so sorry, I never meant it to happen like this. It was the Saturday morning after your date wit him, you'd fallen asleep on the sofa and I got his number from your phone and called him. I just thought him being a model would be the perfect place to start with it all."

"But…. why did you keep it from me?"

"I had to keep it a secret to make sure it didn't get back to Jamie. He would've made sure it didn't happen and I really wanted to see what would come from it, if anything. Jane, I hated lying to you but you have to understand why I did it!"

All she could see was that her best friend had betrayed her. Gone behind her back and lied to her. Her head was swirling with all the new information. Libby had been in contact with Ben even after his attack on Andrew. She'd met with him, concocted this life changing plan with him and was hoping to go over to where he lived and what, move there?

"What if you actually get a job though? You'd be moving to Paris right?"

"It might not even come to that…..but yes…I would have to move out there IF I got any work."

"What about me?"

"This is all happening at the worst time I know. When I started planning, Love Games was doing really well. I had no idea *this* was going to happen."

"So is that everything now, no more secrets?"

A look was passed between the three of them. How could there be more? Jane wasn't sure she could handle anything else. Her heart was breaking but her head was longing for that missing piece of information for any of this to make sense.

"I can cancel or re-arrange though if you need me here" She was upset this was all happening when her life was falling apart and she really needed her friend by her side but she couldn't stop her from going could she! This was her dream, she had to follow it.

"Don't be silly, you go I will be fine." Libby looked at her like she didn't believe a word she was saying but knew better than to argue with her, especially today.

"I just don't like to think of you being here on your own, with all this going on, that's all."

"Well, if you girls have things in order then we should be off. Graham do you want to go down and bring the car around?" Her dad stood immediately, obviously glad to be getting out of the tension filled flat. He walked over to Jane and gave her one of his legendary hugs before going silently out the front door. Her dad's hugs could cure anything from a grazed knee to a broken heart, but sadly they couldn't fix her business and right now she wasn't sure if even she could.

After an emotional exit from her mum, she turned to face Libby. She was just staring at her expectantly but Jane couldn't face looking at her. All she wanted was peace and quiet to try and sort out the complete mess that was in her head.

"Libby, I can't do this right now. I'm shattered. I'm just going to head to bed if that's ok with you?" Not even waiting for a response, she started walking towards her bedroom door. As she reached for the handle she turned back.

"Hey, what time are you leaving for Paris tomorrow?"

"My flight is at 9am so I will be up early. Jane, I know there is more to all this than you are letting on. I think I kind of get it and if I am right then I want you to remember that if two people are meant to be together, then they will eventually find their way back to one another."

Jane stopped dead. How had Libby picked up on it? She was sure she'd concealed her feelings well, but here was Libby giving her advice on something she'd never admitted out loud to anyone. She couldn't bear to admit them to herself let alone say them to anyone else. She offered her a weak smile and quickly made her way inside.

CHAPTER 22

Andrew finished his meeting later than he'd wanted to. All he could think about throughout the presentation was that he was going to be working for another bunch of pretentious bastards. Didn't they realise there was more to life than hosting the most rock and roll party for a bunch of people that didn't give two shits about them, who would only be there for the free booze and free publicity, nothing more?

He despised people who were only famous because they flaunted themselves in the public eye and partied hard because of it. They didn't have any talent, they hadn't given anything back to the world, so why did the public love everything about them? Guess that was where he showed his age. He didn't get it and probably never would.

He'd found it hard to stay focussed after the call from Jane, aware that he had been the one to ensure she worked for him, but she'd been so abrupt. All he could think about was how much he wanted to call her back and tell her the truth. The fact that ever since he had met her, nothing else had been worth thinking about. But he knew she would want to give 'them' a try and he didn't want her to end up resenting him.

He'd been thinking hard after his liaison with her, trying to figure out what was really holding him back. It all boiled down to the fact that he didn't want to hurt her, not that he would do it intentionally. No, he wasn't a prick who would sleep around at the drop of a hat. But because of who he was there was always going to be stories about him and regardless of if they were true or not it was sure to leave cracks in their relationship. Then one day enough would be enough and they would break up.

That and the fact that there wasn't a woman out there who would be happy to spend so much time on her own due to his demanding work schedule. Sure they would love the lifestyle he was able to provide, but he wouldn't be there to share it with her a lot of the time. It was hard to admit to himself as these had been the reasons Carol had given for her affair. Her words had rooted themselves into his brain like a tumour, niggling away in the background whenever he so much as thought about getting close to another woman. He hadn't really been aware of them until now, until he met someone that actually made him question his actions.

It was strange considering it was *her* who had destroyed *him* by cheating, that she'd managed to talk it round so that the onus was on him. *He* was now the reason behind it and that kind of psychological warfare played havoc with your self esteem. More so than he'd understood until now.

Since meeting Jane, he'd been off his game and had made some foolish decisions at work. All he could think about was her and searching the depths of his soul to work out what, and why, he was holding back. He knew he wasn't able to be the man she'd want him to be, he didn't think he had it in him, not now. His work was his life and that was that.

He did feel for her after the article in today's paper. It was obvious she hadn't read it when she'd spoken to him earlier, but an article like that was sure to have earned itself some painful backlash for her business. He knew better than most not to believe what was written in the papers and she had come through for him. He had his date tonight to prepare for so as far as he was concerned she'd done her job and in quick time too.

"Rebecca, I will be leaving early tonight, I have reservations at 8pm." He didn't even stop at her desk, just continued towards his office. She was still pretty pissed at him after their previous altercation, but after a carefully fought argument she had agreed to come back with a 5% payrise, and 1 weeks extra holiday a year. He should have expected her to drive a hard bargain after the eight years she'd worked for him, she had a knack for getting what she wanted. He realised he would do anything to keep her and her upcoming nuptials were making him nervous so he had to try even harder to keep her happy.

"No problem, do you need me to arrange anything for you?"

"No, Ja..ah Miss Aldrin has made the necessary arrangements thank you."

"Oh wow, that was quick. Did you see the paper yesterday? I am not sure she will still have a business after today, poor girl." He chose not to answer, just stepped into his office. Shutting the door behind him, his eyes darted to the little round glass table which he hadn't been able to get rid of. He thought back to that day, his mouth twitching as he remembered how good she'd felt around him. Her smell had invaded all his senses and it had taken hours for it to fade. When it had gone completely, he found himself missing it. This was dangerous territory even for him.

"No, stop it!" He cursed himself and shook his head, trying to shake away the memories. She was going to be very hard to get out of his head, too hard. He hoped he was going to have the strength to stay away from her, it really would be the best thing all round....wouldn't it?

~

It was 7.45pm and Andrew was just pulling up outside the restaurant. He hated being late, but even he thought it would look a bit keen arriving a whole fifteen minutes early. There was also the fact that he would have to wait alone until she arrived and who knows who could be watching him, eager for another story.

"We'll just wait here a moment Tony, I'm a little early" He called through to his driver. Maybe she would arrive while he was waiting and would be able to see what she looked like from a distance. As he sat back his mind thought over the events of the day.

He thought about what Rebecca had said, it was true Jane probably wouldn't be able to come back from this on her own and he really did feel for her. She'd worked hard on her own to build her business up to the highest standard and one little dick had made it all crumble from beneath her, he couldn't have that.

He'd called down to his solicitor a few floors below to work something out. He needed a plan to get Love Games back up and running. Obviously it would need changes so people felt they could put their trust in it again, but he didn't have to sort out those minor issues. He didn't have hundreds of people working for him for nothing.

Having now gotten a small team on the second floor working hard to put a few proposals together for the future of Love Games, he felt he could invite her over to pitch them to her when she was ready. There was still a chance she might surprise everyone and sort it out herself, but his gut feeling was that she would crumble under the pressure. It wasn't necessarily a bad thing...for him anyway. The thought of her moving into his building made him giddy with excitement.

Realising he'd been totally absorbed in his thoughts, it was now nearly 8.05pm and he hadn't been keeping an eye on the door.

"Shit!" He rushed out the car and headed towards the restaurant.

"Excuse me I have a reservation at 8pm, I'm a little late has my date arrived?"

"Let me just check sir, what was the name?"

"Mr B..sorry Mr Smith."

"It looks like your date has just been seated. Follow me." He could feel his hands getting clammy, it was as if he was suffocating inside his suit. He had no idea what to expect, it was the first blind date he'd been on since Carol and look how that had turned out.

He pulled at the neck of his shirt which felt like it was trying to constrict his airways. Jane had said they appeared perfect for each other. Maybe that was the reason for his nerves. *Christ, how far away are we seated?* he thought.

"Surely we should be there by now!" He mumbled behind the waitress' back. He looked around, the place wasn't huge so why was it taking so long to get to his seat? That was when he saw her.

She had her back to him but he could make out a blonde bob which looked like it'd been cut using a spirit level. The line was perfectly straight. She was wearing a fitted dress in the palest of pinks. From what he could see of her there was a good figure beneath it. They were right behind her now and he was moments away from seeing her face.

The waitress halted and announced his arrival. She stood and turned to greet him, wearing a huge smile that immediately dropped as her eyes took in who was standing before her.

"You?" She looked horrified.

"I'm going to give you two a few moments. I'll be back over to take any orders shortly." The waitress, sensing the tension, made her excuses to leave.

"I was told I was meeting Mr Smith! What is going on?"

He couldn't speak. His feet had seemingly become one with the ground making him unable to escape. He wasn't sure whether to laugh or shout . Was this Jane's idea of a sick joke?

"Carol!!? I was under the impression I was meeting Caroline Evans." He showed no emotion, he didn't want to give her the satisfaction of knowing that her mere presence was affecting him.

"I *am* Caroline Evans. It's my pen name. And Mr Smith?"

"So you finally got round to getting your work published?" He hadn't seen his ex-wife for eight years and once the initial shock of seeing her had worn off he realised he was intrigued to know what she'd been up to. She was the last person in the world he wanted to be with right now, especially having a date with, but he thought it might give him some information he could use against her at some point.

"Yeah I have been working on it for years but I guess it finally paid off. So are you going to tell me why you are posing as Mr Smith or is it going to be a fun guessing game?" She relaxed and sat back down motioning for him to join her.

He wasn't sure he was going be able to do this after all. His feet still rooted to the spot beneath him. Gathering all his strength he used all his willpower to lift his feet and make his way towards the empty chair sitting opposite the only woman he had ever despised.

Unbuttoning his suit jacket he managed to regain control of his body and sat down. She seemed normal with him, like no time had passed. Had she forgotten how much she'd hurt him? This was going to be tough, but he wouldn't give up just yet. Knowing Jane would be getting paid if the date was completed was the only thing keeping him there. He knew how much she needed this and he wanted to do everything he could to help her. Even if it meant having a date with his ex wife.

"Not that it's any of your business, but I didn't want anyone to know it was me. I am looking for someone that wants me, not my huge bank account." His eyes flashed a knowing look in her direction. Carol loved money, she thrived on it, the more the better. The only problem was that she wasn't prepared to wait for it, hence her affair. A choice she must have regretted every day since he'd made it big.

"I must admit the first thing that crossed my mind when I saw it was you, was how does Blakey need help finding a date? From what I remember about you and from the stories that keep me up-to-date with your life, I would've thought you had no trouble whatsoever." She was smirking. She knew he hated that nickname, she'd given it to him when they first started dating, long before he was hugely successful. Hearing it after all this time took him back. Back to the time he'd shared with her, the fun they'd once had, but along with it the immense, excruciating pain she'd caused him. She looked like she was enjoying making him feel uncomfortable as she kept going, waiting for him to bite.

"So, tell me…. exactly how much of it is true Blakey?"

"DON'T call me that!" He snapped back at her, wiping the smile from her face.

"You lost the right to call me that a long time ago!"

"Sorry, old habits. It's….. well it's been a long time hasn't it?" Sensing his mood she thought better than to bait him any further.

"You knew me well enough to know what would be true and what wouldn't, or maybe you never knew me at all." The dislike he had for this woman was undeniable. Scanning the room he wondered if people around them could pick up on the hostility emanating from him.

"So, what have you been up to then Bla..sorry Andrew?" Thankful she'd corrected herself this time, he wasn't sure that hearing it again would have any other effect other than him walking out.

"Excuse me. Can I get you both anything to drink?" The waitress had returned at some point while he was surveying the room.

"Carol?" He knew exactly what she was going to order. He would've bet his whole business on the fact that she wouldn't have changed in all the years they'd been apart.

"Cosmopolitan please." *Bingo, there it is. She still must think she is Carrie Bradshaw then.* It was amusing to him, watching her now, knowing he didn't have to take her home with him or in fact ever see her again.

He could remember the countless times he'd gotten in late from work to find her curled up on the sofa with the Sex and the City box set cracked open, re-living over and over again the twisted love story. He thought back to when the film had come out and how thankful he'd been that his marriage had ended. The idea of being dragged to sit through two hours of that shit was too much to comprehend.

"JD on the rocks please, make it a double." Any form of intoxication this evening was needed.

"Really? Wow, guess time has changed you then." He'd never been much of a drinker, he would have the occasional glass of wine with a dinner out but rarely had anything outside of that. As the business had grown so had the stress, so on more than one occasion he'd lost himself in a bottle or two after a tough day.

"Well it had to have an effect on one of us."

"Ouch!" She mocked pain in her heart but was still smiling at him. *Does she think this is a joke or something?*

"So, why a dating agency then Carol? Did it not go as planned with…him?" He couldn't bear to say the name of the good for nothing bastard who'd taken his wife from him.

"No, believe it or not he cheated on me. Guess Karma has a way of getting you back doesn't it?"

In his head he was laughing and applauding the fact that the woman who'd completely destroyed him had felt a bit of what she had done to him first hand. But even that wasn't enough to give him closure.

He took in her appearance properly for the first time since sitting down. She looked alright for her age, but the signs were there she was getting old, which she'd desperately tried to cover.

He noted the dark circles under her eyes and the vast amounts of concealer layered on top in order to disguise them. She was getting wrinkles too. He could see them around her eyes, her forehead and her mouth, no amount of make-up was able to hide those. Just by looking at her he had answered his own question. She was getting old and no-one wanted an old woman.

"It's good to see you Andrew…" She had a contented look in her eyes as she addressed him. Her sudden change in composure made him uneasy. He didn't trust this woman and he didn't like where this seemed to be heading.

CHAPTER 23

"Who does she fucking think she is?" He stormed out of the restaurant with clenched fists and jumped into the back of his car, thankful Tony had opted to wait outside rather than cruise around until he was called for. *How could she even have suggested it? Was she totally out of her mind?*

His driver, a bit taken aback by the sudden entrance of his boss, took a minute to realise what was going on.

"Take me to the club!" He needed a drink. He couldn't ever remember feeling as angry as he did right now. Even when he'd found Carol shagging …him, he'd felt more numb than angry. Knowing his only option was to get out of there he'd made the swiftest of exits, not even leaving his share of the bill. *Fuck her, she deserves to pay for it all,* he thought.

Pulling up outside Marilyn's he didn't even wait for the car to come to a complete stop before jumping out and racing inside. Taking over this place was one of the best decisions he'd ever made, but man did he need to do something about the name.

Why anyone would choose to name their bar after a woman was beyond him. They were nothing but trouble. Heading straight for his office he flung his suit jacket on the back of his chair before dropping down himself.

Resting his head in his hands he took several deep breaths before looking at the computer monitors fixed on the wall. They gave him access to every inch of the club without having to leave the confines of his plush office. It was thanks to them he'd known Jane was there the night he was attacked, and how he had suddenly appeared in the bar for her to see him. He just wished that woman hadn't decided to try and hit on him the very moment she spotted him.

Carol's last words to him flashed back into his thoughts.

"I think we should give it another go Blakey!"

They were echoing round his head so much he wondered if he'd heard her correctly. Surely she wouldn't have the nerve to even think that, let alone say it out loud? But this was Carol, a law unto herself so she was pretty much capable of anything as far as he was concerned.

But seriously! Give it another go? After all this time! She didn't know anything about him now. Eight years is a long time to be apart from someone, he'd changed more than most people would have, he'd certainly changed more than her. No, it was the worst idea he'd ever heard. She had screwed him up too much already. Not only would he always have trust issues, he now couldn't let himself commit to a woman, even to one he could see a future with because of her.

He took another glance at the computer screens to see what wannabe's were in tonight. It was relatively quiet. There were the usual high class business men in waiting for their titty show. Another part of the club he hated, but it had been part of the takeover clause that it had to stay and, he hated to admit it, it did pull in a lot of business. As soon as the time lapsed on that clause it was going to be the first thing to go. He didn't want tits bouncing around in his face when he had a drink, and the perverts that did should find a proper strip club to go to.

He was stopped mid thought and was drawn to the centre monitor. The image shown was in the main bar. He rubbed his eyes. *It couldn't be... could it?* He couldn't really make out the face so couldn't be 100% sure. It might just be someone that looked similar.

He felt compulsion flow through his veins, taking over all his senses.

He had to find out.

Throwing open his door and marching out, he was on a mission and he wouldn't stop until he knew for sure.

***

"Jane, I'm sorry for earlier, it wasn't very nice. You were just *so* clueless. I mean how can someone avoid the headlines all morning?" *Was that an actual apology from William? She'd* heard it all now. It almost made her forget about her deep depression and she even allowed herself to crack a smile.

"It's fine. You were just being…well you!" She couldn't hold it back, she laughed so hard it made her belly hurt. It made her realise it'd been a long time since anything had been this funny.

"Anyway, you have made it up to me by bringing me here, I never really got to explore the place last time."

"Well I did wonder if you would want to come back, Jamie told me what happened last time. But I thought I would mention it, see how the ground lay and all that."

"No no, it was just what I needed. Libby has locked herself in her room to pack for Paris and her fancy ass meetings, with all the shit I've had to deal with today I just needed to get out. How is Jamie by the way?" She threw her drink back thinking another would be brought over like last time. William obviously wasn't as well known in there as Ben as it took a while longer before her cocktail was replenished. She'd noted the lack of champagne too, but still, she couldn't complain, it was a free night out after all.

"He is taking the break-up pretty bad. I don't think he's shaved since he last saw her. She did kind of go to town on him from what I heard."

"I don't think she said anything maliciously. She was just getting off her chest how she'd been feeling."

"I think she acted like a bitch if you ask me."

"Well good job no-one did. Look, neither of us were there so we can't comment on how it was. As far as she was concerned she was just telling him the truth. Now excuse me, I have to go to the ladies room."

Rifling through her clutch as she walked meant she wasn't looking at where she was going.
BANG
She crashed right into someone.

"Oh my gosh I am so sorry.." Tailing off when she looked up and saw who was standing in front of her. Her heart rate increased.

"Andrew...I..." She wasn't sure what to say when something dawned on her.

"Wait, what are you doing here?"

"Jane, it *is* you. Why shouldn't I be here?"

"Of course it's me?! But what about Caroline? Oh God, you didn't stand her up did you?" She was panicking. *Had* he stood her up? Had *she* stood *him* up? Perhaps she'd read the article and decided not to go after all. With so much going round in her brain she couldn't disguise the fact that she was freaking out. Her breathing was raspy and her voice had a hint of deliriousness to it. People around them were starting to stare but she didn't care. If this had all gone wrong, well that was it! It was over, she was finished! What was she going to do now?

"Jane...Jane! JANE! Calm down..... please. We did meet. Jane!" It seemed to get her attention.

"I don't know how to say this but...." *Oh god, what is he going to say? Have I fucked up again?* Feeling a tight sensation in her chest and her breathing quicken once again, she didn't want to have a panic attack in front of him so turned and pushed her way into the bathroom.

What was happening to her? She'd always been so strong, nothing would phase her, now look at her. The first glimmer of anything going remotely wrong and she was staving off panic attacks left, right and centre. Libby was always the one that over-reacted in these kind of situations yet she seemed to be the only one coping between the two of them. When did the roles reverse?

Splashing water on her face, she relished feeling the cold spatter against it. It seemed to have the calming effect she'd hoped it would. The looming panic attack was subsiding and she was no longer on the verge of tears, but there was something still niggling away in the back of her mind.

She spent a few more minutes composing herself before deciding now was the time to make her exit.

"Shit!" She muttered as she saw him. He was still there. Thankfully he had his back to the door so hadn't seen her walk out. It wasn't until the door banged shut behind her that he was alerted to someone standing behind him. He instantly span around.

"Jane, I need to explain. Tonight with Carol. Well It turns out...." She tried to push past him.

"Andrew I can't do this, not now." She didn't want to hear how wrong she'd gotten it once again. What she wanted was to get back to her seat, drink her drink, and hundreds more on top of it.

"Caroline is my ex-wife!" He called after her. The words made her stop dead in her tracks. It was as if she had been punched in the stomach. She had no breath to respond to him, she couldn't even turn to face him. She'd just put the last nail in the coffin with this almighty fuck up!

~

Sliding back into the booth, she finished what was left in her glass and looked around for someone to bring her another. William looked at her with wide eyes but wasn't concerned about her, he actually seemed impressed. He even laughed out loud when the next drink arrived at the table and she drank that one back in one go too.

"Wow, you thirsty or something?"

"Yeah, or something." She replied curtly.

"Has something happened?" She knew he didn't care. Having never been around her for this long he was having to use what little knowledge he had about social conventions to make small talk and feign concern. She'd already made her mind up she was going to go home with him tonight, she knew she wouldn't be able to face Libby leaving the next morning. So he really didn't need to force the idle chit chat. He should know her by now to know she was a sure thing.

She rolled her eyes, he seemed to understand and didn't press the conversation any further.

"Hey, wanna dance?" Finishing off yet another drink and a cheeky shot that'd appeared before her, she nodded at him and jumped out of her seat.

He steered her into the R and B room which was pumping music so loud she couldn't hear him when he turned to speak to her. She didn't care what he had to say, she just wanted to get lost in the beat.

He motioned towards the women gyrating against men around them in perfect time to the beat. She strode in and let herself get swept away by the surge of people on the dance floor. She wasn't aware of the circle of men closing in around her as she danced. She couldn't even tell if William was still with her. She really didn't care at this point, the only thing that mattered was the music.

The room started spinning, or was she literally spinning, she didn't know? The effects of the alcohol had started kicking in and she knew this would probably be the last thing she could remember if she had any more. That was what she intended to do regardless of how it was going to affect her tomorrow.

Knowing she would have the hangover from hell, she realised she no longer cared. It wasn't as if she had a job to go to in the morning. For the first time since reading the article she admitted that it was all over. She'd lost everything. She couldn't have the man she wanted and her business was in ruins, there was no point to anything anymore.

CHAPTER 24

Libby awoke bright and early the next morning. She'd been packing like crazy for most of the night, making sure she had her best designs to go along with the collection she'd had made up. Then there was the task of deciding what to wear herself. She wanted to show off her best pieces, but a lot of them weren't really suitable attire for a formal meeting.

Eventually she found she was able to mix some of her own designed dresses with suit jackets to make herself look professional and still show off her work. She felt really bad that all this was happening when things were so dreadful for Jane. She'd heard her sneak out last night and had either come in when she'd finally gone to sleep, or she hadn't made it home at all.

Creeping down the corridor and slowly opening the door to Jane's room she was faced with an empty bed. One that had most definitely not been slept in. Sighing, she realised that she wasn't going to be there to see her off. She prayed that nothing bad had happened to her, remembering the last time she had gone on a crazy night out. But at least then she'd had someone with her.

"Jane, just checking you are alright. I will be leaving for the airport real soon, hope you are ok."

This was the first of many voicemails she would leave her over the course of the morning before heading to the airport. She told herself she had to try and forget what Jane was going through, she needed to get in the right frame of mind. She was doing all this to follow her dream. She knew Jane would understand eventually.

After checking in her bags and heading to the departure lounge she went to get some breakfast, but the butterflies in her stomach were making her feel sick so she opted for a coffee instead. This was it, she was finally going to be able to pitch her work face to face.

Knowing this was her only chance, she had to give it everything. If she didn't succeed this time, she would be forced to follow the route her parents had mapped out for her. The humiliation of having to go and admit they were right was too much to comprehend. She would do this and wouldn't let anything get in her way.

Seeing her plane was now boarding she popped one last text over to Jane,

Sweetie I'm getting on the plane. I love you x

Taking a deep breath and switching her phone to airplane mode, she joined the queue that had now formed to get on the plane. Feeling her legs shaking in the 6 inch heels she'd decided to wear, she knew she was nervous as hell about this adventure but intended to do everything in her power to get what she wanted. It was her time to shine.

***

Jane slowly prised her eyes apart, but the harsh light streaming around her made her shut them again. She felt like she was dying a slow and painful death. Her mouth was so dry she wondered if she'd been eating sawdust all evening. If it hadn't been for the grumbling noises in her stomach that showed her no food had actually passed her lips for almost twenty four hours, she might have believed that's what she had in-fact been doing.

How stupid was she? She knew alcohol was a bad idea on an empty stomach, even more so for a rookie drinker like her. She tried to prise her head from the pillow. Even though she hadn't managed to get her eyes open again she saw the room spinning and felt like she was going to keel over.

Shuffling to a semi-seated position she plucked up the courage to open an eye. It wasn't as bright as their first exposure suggested, so she was able to safely open the other without a piercing pain shooting through her head. As soon as her eyes were able to focus she started to panic.

Where the hell am I? Having never seen this room before she looked around realising that she was completely alone and had absolutely no idea whose bed she was in. *Had William moved? Surely he would have bragged about bagging himself a pad like this.* The bedroom alone was bigger than her entire flat.

Spying an en-suite through an open door she flung her legs over the side of the bed. Even the bed seemed a gazillion times bigger than her double which almost filled her room at home. Her feet didn't even touch the floor, even though she was sitting right on the edge of it.

It had on crisp white linen sheets which, despite having had her sleeping in it, had zero creases whatsoever. Having to do a little jump to get off, she had an amusing image of poor Libby trying to get on. Being so tiny it would be extremely comical to watch her clambering to get her legs up.

Libby! Libby is going to Paris.... today. She had no idea where her bag was and it was only then she realised what she was wearing. A shirt! Not the clothes she'd gone out in which were also no-where to be seen. She searched the room, which despite being so large actually had very little in it.

There were fitted wardrobes along one side which boasted a spectacular mirrored front, a beautifully crafted dressing table on another and the biggest TV she'd ever seen fixed to the wall, angled in the perfect way to watch comfortably from the bed. What confused her was that nothing looked like it had ever been used.

She made her way to the en-suite. It was a wet room and she noted that fresh towels had been left in there along with a new hairbrush, toothbrush and toothpaste. She knew at this point that she wasn't at William's house, he would never be this considerate to a house guest. Her concern about who'd brought her here was now growing rapidly. Feeling herself starting to freak out she scanned the room looking for any answers. It was then she noticed a white robe hanging behind the door with a note pinned to it.

Jane, you are safe. Have a shower, get freshened up and come and meet me in my office. Take your time.

There was no indication as to who had left the note or what office she was meant to meet them in. She wasn't going to leave this room without any clothes that was for sure.

The shower did look inviting so she peeled off the shirt. It smelt good, unlike her who smelt like a brothel, and like the bed it barely had a crease on it. Hooking her fingers into her pants she slipped them down and unhooked her bra.

Standing under the shower head she turned it on, feeling invigorated as the hot water beat down on her face. While she showered she came up with so many ideas as to where she could be, but deep down knowing she was too scared to go and actually find out. She decided to stay as long as she possibly could in the shower where she felt safe.

It wasn't long before it felt like her skin was shrivelling up from being in the water for so long. She couldn't stay in there for a second more so turned off the water and wrapped herself in a towel. It was the softest towel she'd ever felt, which having been hung on the heated towel rail, made it nice and cozy. She just wanted to curl back up in bed and sleep, but knew she had to find out where she was and most importantly where her phone was. She'd missed Libby, the clock told her it was now 9.30am, she would be in the air on her way to Paris by now, but she could at least leave her a message.

Stopping dead in her tracks as she re-entered the bedroom, three bags had appeared on the bed. There was no indication where they had come from or who had put them there. She slowly crept over to them. Her eyes searching for any sign there was someone, anyone, there. Relaxing slightly as she concluded she was in-fact alone. Getting closer to the bags she couldn't believe where they were from. *This has to be a joke! Chanel, Agent Provocateur and Christian Louboutin. No! These can't be for me.* Spotting another note she snatched for it and read it eagerly;

I thought you might like a change of clothes. Apologies if I got the sizes wrong I had to guess some of it.

Not sure what to make of any of this, she peeked into one of the bags, expecting it to be filled with toy snakes or some other novelty item. It wasn't the case and she gasped as she pulled out a dress and cardigan from Chanel. They were exactly her size and looked more expensive than the entire contents of her wardrobe. Okay so it was just a simple black dress, but the fabric felt so soft she couldn't wait to slip into it, regardless of how rubbish she felt. The cardigan was the real version of the replica one she had purchased not too long ago.

Looking next in the Agent Provocateur bag she pulled out a pretty matching set in black lace. Even though whoever had got it for her could've had no idea what size she was, they'd gotten it spot on. Glancing around the room yet again just to make sure she was alone, she slipped out of the robe and tried it on. The soft lace clung to her skin and unlike all her other underwear, felt as if she wasn't wearing anything. She slipped the dress over her head and secured the zip. She finally understood Libby's passion for clothes. Never had she felt so good just by wearing something so beautiful.

Finally she got the shoes out of the last bag, almost groaning in delight when she saw that they were the classic black patent style with that legendary red sole. Slipping them onto her feet they felt like they had been made especially for her. Giving her damp hair a quick brush she wished she had some make-up with her, she knew that now was the time to exit the room. She had to find the person that had done this for her, and as why. It was now or never.

Opening the door slowly, just in-case there was someone waiting outside, she peered out into a very white corridor with many more doors along it. *Is this a hotel? No, there aren't any number on the doors so it can't be.* It was then she heard a noise. It was coming from behind one of the doors.

Deciding she simply had to know where she was and get her things back, she headed towards it. Feeling awkward, she cautiously knocked before opening. The door led her into a massive open plan kitchen and living area. Everything was clinically white, and where possible, was made of glass. She was in complete awe as her eyes scanned the room trying to take it all in. It was then that she noticed the small squat woman busying herself cleaning. Hoping to get some answers she made her way towards her.

"Ah, excuse me?" Her voice came out husky and was barely audible. She remembered she hadn't drank anything yet so coughed and tried again.

"Excuse me?" It seemed to have gotten her attention, but she did appear shocked she was being addressed at all.

"Yes dear?" She asked back cautiously, glancing over to a closed door on the other side of the room.

"Could you please tell me where I am?" The question sounded ridiculous even to her, but thankfully the lady didn't seem to think so. She smiled and pointed to the closed door.

"He is in there. He asked me to get you something to eat before sending you in." She started towards the kitchen as soon as she'd said it.

"I'm not hungry!" Jane lied. She just wanted to know where she was and who had done all this for her. All she could now be sure of, thanks to this woman, was that it was in fact a he.

"I am not to take no for an answer. How you like your eggs?" She wasn't going to be able to get out of this one.

"Scrambled…please. " Well she had to go with how her brain felt didn't she?

As soon as she swallowed her first mouthful her stomach grumbled in delight, the first thing to enter it that wasn't in liquid form. These had to be the best scrambled eggs she'd ever tasted and she savoured each blissful mouthful as she devoured the whole lot in seconds. She sipped on her freshly squeezed orange juice and was shocked at how much better it tasted this way, rather than the crappy cartons her and Libby always had.

With her thoughts returning to Libby, she realised she still had no idea where any of her things were. She desperately needed to find her phone and make sure she'd got to the airport ok.

"Excuse me, sorry I don't your name.." She blushed, she'd accepted this amazing food from this little woman and hadn't bothered to ask what her name was.

"Mrs Barker dear, was there something else you needed?" She nodded towards her empty plate.

"Oh no, no more food thank you. I just wondered if you knew where my things were?"

"In there." She pointed towards the office door she'd shown her earlier. So whoever was in there must really want to see her and not just have her get her things and slip away without speaking to him.

"Can I go in and get them? I really should be getting home, I have a lot to sort." *I need to get my life back in order and sort out what's left of my business!*

Mrs Barker looked at the clock on the wall. Jane's eyes followed her gaze. It was 9.55am.

"Five more minutes, he should be ready for you then"

Hearing a click in the kitchen, her senses were suddenly hit with the strong smell of freshly brewed coffee. It intoxicated her and made her mouth water with longing. Mrs Barker stopped cleaning the large lamp she'd been tending to and went back into the kitchen. She set to work preparing a tray with two cups and saucers, a small selection of biscotti and finally the coffee. She nodded at her and although no words were exchanged she knew it must now be 10am. Time to meet the mysterious man that appeared to have kidnapped her and given her an amazing designer make-over. She wasn't sure if she should be angry with him or thanking him. The confusion mixed with her hangover was making her feel dizzy.

She stood and smoothed out her fabulous dress. Loving how the fabric felt on her skin as she moved, hearing the click clack of her killer heels, she followed Mrs Barker like a lost puppy across the lounge. Her heart thudding inside her chest.

This was it.

She was going to meet him.

Mrs Barker knocked.

She could make out some shuffling from the other side but there was no speaking.

She wanted to run but knew she didn't stand a chance in those heels, plus she needed her phone back so she had to go in.

The handle began turning.

The door was opening slowly.

She still couldn't see who it was. Her view was obscured by Mrs Barker as she entered with the tray of coffee.

Then she saw him.

The mysterious man who hadn't wanted her to leave without first seeing him.

So, here she was in Andrew Blake's apartment, standing in clothes he'd bought her and totally confused as to why.

CHAPTER 25

Holy shit she looks good, was all he could think when he laid eyes on her. He could feel a twitch in his trousers, but managed to maintain control and stop his eyes from wandering. This was simply business, it had to be.

"Good morning, I hope you weren't too confused when you woke up?"

"Well I was… very actually. I had no idea where I was and I couldn't find any of my things. Safe to say I've had better mornings." She hadn't meant to be so aggressive but he'd been so secretive and as far as she was concerned it all seemed totally unnecessary.

"I'm sorry to have alarmed you, but I wanted to make sure you were in the right frame of mind before we spoke this morning."

"I just need my things!"

"And you will get them but first, sit down. Coffee?"

Without waiting for her reply he nodded at Mrs Barker who poured out two cups and left them neatly on the desk. Jane blinked and she'd gone. She could just make out the faint click of the door as it was pulled shut behind her.

"Please sit." Obediently she did and looked up at him, her concern growing with each second that passed. Gauging the situation, she concluded that something had happened. She tried desperately to recall the events of last night, but the last thing she could clearly remember was dancing…..then nothing. It was as if someone had broken inside her head and stolen all her memories from that point onwards.

"It's nothing, please don't look at me like that."

"Andrew, what's this about? What happened last night? How did I end up here?"

He obviously hadn't banked on having to explain it all straight away. He didn't want to re-live the events that had brought her there, he wanted to forget all of it. He just wanted to get down to business, that's where he felt most comfortable.

"Oh…Of course. Well, you drank a lot and refused to stop, much to my annoyance. You got into….. how to put it…a sticky situation. Your male friend left you while he copped off with one of my dancers. I helped out and didn't want to leave you alone in the state you were in, so I brought you here. I hope that was the right thing to do?"

"What situation? What could possibly be so bad that made you act all knight in shining armour for me, the last time we spoke…well.." Her brows were knotted together, she was trying with all her might to find any memory in the vast blank space that was the remainder of the evening.

"Lets just say there were some unsavoury characters in my club last night and you got caught in the middle of them. They will not be allowed to step foot in there again after what they almost did." The look on her face told him she wasn't going to leave it there, she needed to know more.

"Jane, I stopped you from getting…."
"What is it Andrew? Just spit it out!"
"Raped…I stopped you from getting raped Jane."
Bang, there it was, a look he never wanted to see on her pretty face.

"What?" Her mouth remained open in sheer amazement to what he'd just told her. There was a hint of disbelief creeping into her eyes.

"I wish it wasn't true. Your dancing attracted quite a lot of attention and you allowed yourself to be taken to a dark corner with a couple of men who then wouldn't take no for an answer. If I hadn't been watching you on the CCTV…… who knows what would have happened….." He trailed off not wanting to think about the consequences of him not intervening.

He'd struggled with the image all night of Jane trying to fight the two men off but simply not having the strength to. Her dress had been hitched up and her pants were about to be ripped off. He'd only just gotten there in time to stop it going any further. He'd never punched anyone before and although it was surprisingly satisfying, he quickly realised that punching someone really bloody hurt! Without realising, he massaged his sore hand. Jane watched him and noticed his swollen red knuckles.

"What did you do? Are you alright? I….I can't believe it" She was shaking her head and was at a complete loss as to what to say to him. It was all a bit much to get her head around.

"I did what what I had to do. But, you are ok thankfully and I got you some new clothes so you don't have to remember any of it. I just… I had to know you were alright."

"I think I am….. thanks to you anyway." She looked at him with such sincerity, he just wanted to cup her face and kiss her to make everything better. Knowing he couldn't get involved with her didn't stop the longing. He'd never craved anything more in his life than he did her right at that very moment. *Business Andrew, she is just here for business. He* snapped himself out of his wandering thoughts.

"Now, I have something further I want to discuss with you, if you feel up to it that is?"

She nodded and he walked around to pick up a file from his desk.

"I want to help save your business Jane." He handed it over to her. She took it without even looking at it.

"Andrew, what is this?"

"That right there is the key to saving your business."

***

Did I just hear him right? She thought. After everything she'd just heard, she wasn't sure if her brain was malfunctioning or if she had indeed heard him correctly.

"Sorry…..what?"

"I would like to help you save your business." He sat down opposite her and leaned back in his chair. He looked relaxed, like he did this everyday. *That's cause he does Jane you idiot!*

"I'm sorry I still don't understand?"

"After Neil's article, who has been fired by the way, I made a call and pulled in a few favours so he is no longer employable as a journalist, you might have stood a chance sorting it all out on your own. But now with the subsequent articles in today's paper, there is no way you would be able to continue with Love Games as it stands today."

"Hold on… there have been more? Do you have them? Can I see?"

"I don't think that's a good idea. Lets just say your friend William hasn't exactly helped matters."

William!

She knew something was up last night, he was being too nice to her. He wanted one last piece of the cake before it got taken away from him for good. What had he said about her? She needed to know what the articles said. She needed to get out of here and buy them. All of them so no-one else could see them.

"I have had my team working all night to get the best proposition ready for a take-over ready this morning. You have it right there in your hands. I want you to read it thoroughly and let me know your thoughts. I am ready to hit the transfer button and set the wheels in motion as soon as you give me the green light."

Looking at the folder blankly, she made no attempt to open it. This would need some serious reading and lots of coffee. She was sure it would be the best offer she'd get at this point, but she wasn't sure what the extent of the damage was until she got into the office. She was going to have to check everything before signing any contract. People like Andrew didn't make all their money by being nice in business.

This was all too much to take in, finding out she'd almost been raped, hearing that more people had cashed in on her demise and now this beautiful man wanted to save her. It was all a bit too damsel in distress for her liking and she needed hard facts, and strong painkillers, before making any decisions.

"I have a few things to check first. Err, my things?"

She was relieved that he acted instantly, he moved over to a corner where a bag containing her belongings had been stored. At least he didn't expect her to read it and make a decision there and then. Her brain was even more scrambled than when she first woke up. She would need an IV of coffee slowly drip feeding it to her throughout the day before she'd be able to even consider reading the package she was clutching in her hands.

"Jane, I have made sure all the papers containing articles about you and your business have been removed from sale, please don't waste time looking for any."

How much power did this man have? Despite her feelings, she actually knew very little about him, could she really sign everything over to someone she didn't know? Could she really work for *this* man? Feeling confused she started for the door. The sound of her shoes on the wood floor made her stop and turn back.

"Thank you for the clothes, they are above and beyond what you needed to have done for me. I will pay you back."

"Not necessary, you needed them. Let me know what you think of the proposal. The quicker we move on this the better."

"It's a huge decision. I really don't know what I want right now. My head is just….." She trailed off, unable to even begin to describe how she was feeling.

"One of the hardest lessons in life is letting go. Whether it's guilt, anger, love, loss or betrayal. Change is never easy. This will be the best thing I am sure of it."

She didn't respond, deep down she knew he was right. Walking out his office she waved goodbye to Mrs Barker and headed for the front door. Once again fighting back tears, the full extent of the events over the last 24 hours had finally hit her.

CHAPTER 26

Touching down, Libby was grateful to be back on solid ground. She hated flying so was thankful it was only a short flight. Paris had been everything she dreamed it would be. Despite not having time to do much sight seeing, Ben had made sure she still enjoyed herself. She hadn't realised just how many meetings he'd set up for her until she arrived and saw her itinerary. He'd even gone as far as arranging some models to wear the pieces she'd taken with her.

She left feeling inspired. She'd learnt so much in just 24 hours and for the first time she actually believed she had a chance to get this. She didn't want to get her hopes up too much… just in-case. She wasn't even sure when she should expect to hear from any of them. She prayed it would be sooner rather than later, she didn't know how much her nerves could take.

She hadn't been able to get in touch with Jane while she was away. She knew she was safe after some garbled voicemail she'd left her, not that she'd had the time to listen to it properly or call her back for that matter, but she was thankful to know she was alright. Having managed to squeeze in four appointments that afternoon after arriving before Ben took over the plans for the evening, she'd barely had time to so much as look at her phone let alone use it.

After finally finding her luggage on the carousel she made her way towards the exit to grab a taxi home. It was mid morning and she wasn't sure if Jane would've bothered going into the office or if she'd decided to just give up. Thinking back to the voicemail she recalled something about a business offer, but the line was so rubbish she couldn't be sure if she'd heard it correctly or not.

Settling herself into the taxi, She rested her head back and stared out the window. It was a typical English day, rainy and grey, but her mood was the complete opposite. She felt full of joy and hope, and that for the first time in her life things were moving in the right direction. She had a warm glow inside and knew she was going to be distraught if nothing came from this trip.

Pushing the thought from her mind she watched the scenes of London flashing by through the rain soaked window. Although she was home she'd never felt further from where she believed she was destined to be. Wishing with all her heart she was back in Paris where she felt she belonged. She was quickly distracted from her longing thoughts by the sound of her phone ringing.

***

Jane kept watching the clock, it barely seemed to be moving. The seconds were ticking by and she knew Libby would be home soon and she really needed her friend. This business offer had come as a total shock and the more she thought about it the more she believed it was her only option. It was make or break time and if she chose to break she might never be able to be fixed again.

After reading it through for the hundredth time she could see it really was her only option, and despite her essentially selling to Andrew, she would still be in charge. There were quite a number of 'necessary' changes as the document worded it, and it was these she had some reservations about.

Then there was the issue of her feelings. Even though she didn't understand them, they were still there. Would she be able to work so closely with him without them eventually getting in the way? Hearing her ring tone warbling away, she set out on a mission to find it before it went to voicemail. Regretting not doing any cleaning, which would have made the process much easier, she located it under the sofa. It was an unknown number. She didn't normally answer unknown numbers but it wasn't as it she had anything else to lose by doing so.

"Hello?"

"I's Andrew."

SILENCE

"I just wondered if you had any more thoughts on what we spoke about yesterday?" *Oh God,* just hearing his voice made her insides quiver. He had so much power over her emotions, she was thankful he wasn't aware of it, she knew he had the capability to make her do anything he wanted to.

"Well I still don't know. This is all happening so fast."

"Did you check in at your office?" She'd gone straight there after leaving his apartment yesterday. He'd been right of course, the subsequent articles had put the last bullet right in the heart of her business and she'd resolved herself to the fact that Love Games only had two options left. It could either be dead and buried and she would have to start fresh doing something else or it could be re-incarnated in the form of Andrew's proposal. The hardest part was deciding which option to choose.

"Yes and you were right. Love Games as we know it is over." She shed a single tear, silently leaving a trail of moisture in its wake, she was glad her voice wasn't giving away that she was on the brink of another breakdown.

"I need to talk things over with Libby. Is this the best number to get you on?"

"Yes, this is ah..this is my personal number." Without saying goodbye he hung up just as the door to the flat opened and Libby walked in.

"Jane!!!!!" Libby ran over and threw her arms around her.

"How have you been, I'm sorry if I upset you by going? I missed you! I heard there were more articles. Are you ok? Have you been to the office?"

She sighed and explained everything that'd happened while she had been away. Libby listened open mouthed, there was so much for her to take in.

"Holy shit! So I heard right about the business thing. What are you going to do? Can I see the shoes??" *Trust Libby to get side tracked with fashion at a time like this.*

"Of course." She laughed. The smile felt false on her face after spending the best part of the last day either frowning or crying, but it was certainly a welcomed change.

"Jane...what are you going to do?"

"I still don't know. I just worry I will find it hard working for him when I feel …..I guess I just have to get a few things sorted in here before I can decide." Tapping her head she realised this really wasn't going to be an easy decision to make. She loved her work and wasn't sure what else she'd be able to do if she didn't have it. At the same time she wasn't sure how she would function working alongside him but not being able to emotionally connect with him.

"Jane, have you spoken to him about how you feel? You know every day you wait is another day you won't get back. I think you are going to have to be honest about your feelings with this Hun and then go from there." She'd never mentioned her feelings to Libby but somehow she'd picked up on them. The thought of discussing them with anyone terrified her.

"Do you know what, I'm sick of it always being about me. Tell me about Paris?"

If there was one thing she wasn't ready for it was having to admit she'd fallen for a man she couldn't have. The age difference alone meant they were generations apart, she hated to admit he was probably right in not letting anything happen between them. So why couldn't she let it go?

Libby was acting strange, shuffling around in her seat, her eyes looking everywhere in the flat apart from at her. Something had happened. She'd been upset about Libby heading off to chase her dream, but deep down she wanted her to do well. She wasn't a bitch, she was just human.

"It went really well. I totally loved it over there."

"And…..?" Jane felt tense, she could sense there was something up. Libby was keeping something from her.

"Jane do we have to do this now?"

"Yes we do! What are you not telling me?"

"I just got a call that's all, in the taxi on my way here….."

"AND???? Just get to the point Libby! I'm getting a bit tired of having to force people to tell me things." She was on the verge of shouting, desperate to know what she was hiding from her once again.

"I really don't think now is the….."

"Libby will you just tell me already!"

"FINE! They called and offered me a job! Are you happy now?"

The words hit her with such force they physically took her breath away. Yes, she knew her friend was extremely talented, but after all these years and after all the rejections she'd already faced, she'd been preparing herself to comfort her friend when the inevitable rejection letters filtered through. But they'd offered her a job. This was it. Her best friend, was going to be moving to Paris. She was going to be left all on her own for the first time in forever.

"Wow!"

"I don't have to take it, I can stay here and help you, you know I would do that."

"NO!…..no, I couldn't, I wouldn't let you. Libby this has always been your dream and you deserve it, you've worked so hard, you have to take it, you just….you just have to.." She was unable to hold the tears back. She sobbed out her words and her eyes flooded with the tears she'd been wanting to shed all morning.

"Oh, I am so sorry, this has come at the worst time ever hasn't it? I wish I could change everything for you and make it all better. I'm so so sorry!"

"None of this is your fault, don't worry. You have to do what's best for you and Paris is clearly that." It felt good to be honest with one another. She knew they'd left things on rocky ground the last time they'd been together but after everything that had happened it now seemed pointless and Jane knew she couldn't be angry with her best friend anymore. All she'd done was prioritise herself for the first time in her entire life and gone after something she'd always wanted. She couldn't begrudge her that.

They were both crying, sitting silently on their little sofa in their tiny apartment. Jane finally asked a question that'd been on the tip of her tongue but had been too scared to say out loud. She was terrified of the answer.

"When…ah..when do you have to move?" Libby's face fell even more which Jane hadn't thought could even be possible.

"Here's the shit part. I have to fly back out tomorrow. They want me to start straight away."

TOMORROW? Her head was spinning. She'd expected to have a few weeks at least with Libby before she had to leave. This was all happening so quickly. Too quickly. First the business, then Andrew, now Libby! She was losing everything. Racing to the bathroom she hoisted up the toilet seat and emptied what little contents she had in her stomach down it.

Hearing Libby sobbing in the living room, she knew there was only one choice left for her. Grabbing her phone from her pocket she typed out a simple message;

Andrew, I accept Jx

She didn't have the strength to call him, to have to face the emotions she'd feel just hearing his voice. Almost instantly there was a reply.

This will work out for the best I promise. Meet me at the office 9am tomorrow. Ax

There it was, that confusing kiss. She groaned and buried her head back in the toilet. The sound of her vomiting muted the crying that was still drifting through from her best friend.

"What a way to spend our last night living together!" Jane managed to shout through before cracking up into a fit of hysterical laughter.

CHAPTER 27

It was 7am and Andrew had just arrived at the office. Jane would be there at 9am and he wanted everything ready. This was going to be hard enough for her without the hassle of setting up a whole new office. It was going to be hard for him too spending so much time with her and not letting his feelings get the better of him.

"Rebecca, thank you for coming in early. Have they brought the things from the site in Covent Garden?"

"You owe me. Yes, everything is here. It's been put in the empty office next to yours. I am surprised you didn't want to use one of the vacant spaces in a lower level though?" She smiled a knowing smile in his direction. He decided to swerve the insinuating question and knew a surefire way to get her to go off on a tangent.

"How are the wedding plans going?"

"Oh, really well thank you, we are looking at setting a date. It's proving quite difficult though, you know, finding a time that suits us both."

"Well you can take off as much time as you need you know that."

"Thank you. You know, I will take you up on that."

"Just make sure you do come back at some point!" He laughed nervously although he was deadly serious about making sure she came back, he'd already proved he was willing to do anything to keep her so didn't need to press the point.

Right, time to get the office set up. He opened the door that concealed an office space around half the size of his, but still had the same spectacular view. He'd watched Jane the moment she first saw it. The breathtaking reaction had glowed on her face as she absorbed it all. He wanted to give her that feeling everyday, every time she walked into work. He felt bad that she'd lost everything and had to sell all her hard work. The least he could do was make the transition into a new office as comfortable as possible.

He began setting up the computer on what was now her desk, changing the background to the AB Inc logo like all the others in the building. Love Games would need a whole new name, but this was something he wanted her to be a part of and would be the first task he'd set her that morning, after she'd met everyone and settled in that is.

The other major thing she'd need to get her head around was the new business model. It was based upon being an internet run dating agency. The face to face stuff would be left for the high end clients looking for partners for events. He would have to make it crystal clear it wasn't an escort agency, there would be no funny business, not when his name was attached to it. He had his top marketing guys making sure his vision was put across clearly, all they needed was the name.

Looking up at the small table in the corner, he hadn't been sure if he should put it in here or not. He wasn't sure what reaction she would have seeing it again, but he couldn't have it in his office any longer. He found he spent most of his day just gazing at it remembering what happened when she'd last sat there. He moved it in late last night as soon as he'd heard back from her. It had been the first piece of furniture to go into her new office and he believed it could well be the first to be removed. He would try to gauge her reaction when she arrived.

He spent several minutes setting everything up on her desktop and laptop, then arranged her desk in a way he thought she would like. He wasn't even sure why he was doing any of it. She would want to sort these little things out herself but he found he just couldn't help himself. The next couple of hours were going to drag, he wished he could make the clock hands move quicker so that she'd be there already and he could see her face again.

"Andrew stop it." He muttered aloud to himself.

"You know that's the first sign of madness referring to yourself in the third person."

"I thought it was talking to yourself?"

"Yes that too." She smiled at him as she brought in the huge vase of fresh flowers he'd ordered. She was the only one that knew he'd actually opened an account with the florist so that Jane would have fresh flowers delivered every Monday before she arrived for work.

***

"So is that everything?" Jane asked as she looked at the small amount of luggage Libby had scattered by the door. Considering they'd lived together for so long, Libby didn't really have that much to claim as her own. Seeing as she was pushing thirty it was quite sad to be able to fit your entire life's possessions into 3 suitcases and a holdall, it just didn't seem right somehow.

"Yeah, doesn't seem much does it? This is my life all neatly packed into three bags."

"Neatly?"

"Well, you know…"

Libby looked awkward and for the first time in her life she couldn't find the words to say how she was feeling. They'd been friends for so long that words weren't always needed. A mere look was enough to say what a thousand words simply couldn't. A huge chapter in both of their lives was now coming to an end. They were destined to go their separate ways and start new stories of their own, but knowing this didn't seem to make it any easier.

She felt her stomach knot tight as she fought with all her might to hold it together. She had to stay strong and show Libby she'd be alright on her own. She had a new job herself to begin that very morning and she sure as hell didn't want to screw it up. Feeling bile rising in her throat as the tears threatened to reveal themselves, she distracted herself by answering the intercom.

"Hello?"

"Taxi for Libby"

This was it. Libby was moving and who knew when she'd be able to see her again. Closing her eyes she took a deep breath before she was able to respond.

"Thank you, we will be down in five."

"Li…." She'd started shouting but Libby had already re-appeared from the bathroom which she'd ducked into when things started getting too emotional for her.

"Is it time already?" Noting the crack in her voice tipped her over the edge and she couldn't hold back any longer. All her emotions burst out as if a dam had broken and she had absolutely no control over them. Tears of sadness, tears of joy, tears of pride and tears from her own situation all boiling to the surface and overspilling.

There was a pain in her chest as if her heart was physically breaking. This girl had been with her through everything. Libby was essentially her soul mate and she was now leaving her. Without realising what she was doing she ran to her, threw her arms around her neck and there they just stood for several moments sobbing silently into each others embrace.

The intercom beeped again forcing them to part. She was going to make her late if she kept her up there much longer so, giving her friend a weak smile, she motioned at her that it was time.

She picked up two of the suitcases and carried them into the lift behind Libby. They were both still sobbing, averting their gazes to the corners of the lift. Anything but to have to look each other in the eyes as this was sure to set off a new wave of tears.

At the bottom they were met with an agitated taxi driver who was clearly in a rush to get to his next fare. He didn't speak to either of them, just nodded at Libby and started putting the cases into the back of the cab. She began rustling around in her bag and pulled out her set of keys to the flat, clutching them close to her heart before holding them out for Jane to take.

"Jane, thank you for everything. You have kept me going and without you I would never have been able to do any of this."

Jane hated goodbyes and knew she didn't have the time to say everything she wanted to.

"I love you Lib!" Libby's eyes closed and a single tear dropped onto her cheek. Brushing it away with the back of her hand, she painted on her award winning smile and even managed a soft laugh.

"Christ..Anyone would think we were never going to see each other again. We have mobiles, Skype, and it's only a short flight away. It's not the end, it never could be with us pair."

"Yeah I know, it…..it just will never be the same again will it?"

"Jane, you have a whole new beginning too. This takeover will keep you super busy and then there is Andrew….who knows what will happen there?"

"Nothing, he's made that clear enough."

"I think you should tell him how you feel. If you start out honest with him then you can both go from there. Don't let the grass grow under your feet Hun."

"It's not that easy though is it? He is technically my boss now."

"But if you lay all your cards on the table the worst he could say is no and you know where you stand. Yeah it might be awkward for a bit but at least you guys will be so busy sorting out the business you won't notice it."

Hugging her friend tightly she knew what she had to do.

"Just be honest and go get the man you love!"

Libby got into the taxi and closed the door. Jane was glued to the pavement as she watched her best friend leaving for her new life. She'd just realised the extent of her feelings for him.

She was in love with him.

She'd never admitted to loving any man before, she'd never even come close. How had Libby had seen it before she did?

She loved him.

She had fallen hard the moment their eyes first met.

She was crazy in love with Andrew Blake.

Shit! I'm in love with my new boss!

Groaning, she realised this could all end very badly.

CHAPTER 28

Jane had felt it a tad unnecessary, but he'd insisted on sending a car to pick her up. She hated that she was having to leave her cozy little nook in Covent Garden. It was the place where she'd worked hard for so many years, but she knew he liked all his acquisitions under one roof, and that now included hers.

She wasn't sure what to expect when she arrived and was a mixed bag of emotions as she travelled to the office. She was really cut up about Libby leaving, but now she was nervous about facing Andrew too. The work thing she could sort out, she was a professional business woman after all. But now she knew she was in love with a man who'd made it obvious, on several occasions, that he didn't want her. She wasn't sure how to act around him. She wasn't sure if she would even be able to act normally now she knew the full extent of her feelings. She'd been questioning why people craved to be in love when all it did was made you a nervous wreck.

Pulling up outside she took a moment to check her reflection in her compact. Her eyes were still puffy from crying but she'd managed to re-apply her make-up so she looked half decent at least. She hoped no-one would judge her. Slipping out the car she took a moment to look up at the glass fronted building she was now going to be spending the majority of her days within.

She pulled at the bottom of her jacket to make sure she looked as pristine as she possibly could, then marched her Louboutins through the doors. It wasn't until she'd gotten inside she realised she had no clue where her office was.

She looked around waiting for a sign to appear out of thin air and show her the way. Unsurprisingly nothing did. She felt like turning around and walking right back out when the receptionist she'd met before approached her smiling. That smile alone was the only reason she'd landed herself the front of house job Jane thought.

"Miss Aldrin. So lovely to see you again and to hear you have joined the AB team. Mr Blake has asked me to send you straight up to his office. Can you remember how to get there or shall I call up?"

Of course, he would want to see me first wouldn't he. Why hadn't she realised it wouldn't be as easy as going to her computer and getting stuck in? There would be meetings, tours, all the usual bollocks that accompany a first day in any new office.

"Take the lift straight to the top?"

"You got it. Here is your pass, you will need to keep that on you at all times when in the building. Have a great day." *Well it can't get any worse can it?* She mused but flashed a smile back at the lady who'd saved her the embarrassment of getting lost. She clutched her pass as she headed towards the lifts. This was it, she was going to see him.

As soon as the lift doors opened at the top Rebecca was waiting with coffee and a friendly smile.

"Good morning Miss Aldrin. Mr Blake has appointed me as your assistant alongside him so if there is anything you need just let me know."

Assistant? I have an assistant? Feeling a strange sensation creeping inside her, she found the walk to Andrew's office harder than ever. Her legs seemed to be getting heavier with each step. She told herself everything would be ok, she would get through this..... She had to!

Rebecca returned to her desk and Jane didn't want to ask her for help. Scared that she might end up having another panic attack, she forced herself to move along the corridor smiling as she passed her at her little desk, before coming face to face with Andrew's closed door. This was it. No turning back now.

Knock knock

"Come in!" He answered instantly. Jane cautiously turned the handle. Not knowing how she would feel when she saw him again, she slowly opened the door. There he was, jacket off typing away furiously on his laptop. He was so engrossed in what he was doing he didn't even look up to see who it was. That was until she spoke.

"Good morning Mr Blake."

He froze then closed his laptop and jumped out his chair.

"Jane, I am so sorry I lost track of time. Fussy clients....... How are you?" He looked at her puffy eyes, concern suddenly etched on his face.

"Yes, I'm fine thank you. Libby just left for Paris this morning. She got a job over there so it's been an emotional morning to say the least." She wondered why she was telling him all this, he didn't even know her. He looked like he felt her pain, his brow etched with wrinkles from the frown he was now wearing.

"I'm sorry to hear that. If this is too much for you today we can postpone until tomorrow?"

"No, it will be good to keep busy." She found his eyes and her insides melted. She had thought that when she saw him she might feel differently. Perhaps she was just in love with the idea of falling in love with him. But no, as soon as she saw those ice blue eyes she knew she was in deep. But the question was when to lay her cards on the table?

With so many things racing through her mind she began to feel faint. She wanted to scream at him *I love you can't you see that?* But knew that even if she did it might not make any difference and she'd just be left looking a fool. This would need planning, she had to know exactly what she was going to say to him when the time eventually came.

"So shall we start with a tour of the building before I show you your office?"

"Okay." *NO!* She was screaming inside. *I want to stay here and talk to you! I want to tell you how I feel and beg you to give me a chance. Give us a chance.* She couldn't just come out with it, so followed him obediently out the door.

~

When they finally finished the tour and made their way back up to the top floor her stomach was grumbling loudly. Embarrassed, she glanced at the clock behind Rebecca.
12.30pm.
Lunchtime.

Wondering what time she'd be allowed to escape and grab something to eat, Andrew pointed to a door. She hadn't even noticed it the last time she'd been there but here it was showing off a shiny new sign gleaming on the front. She took a step forward to read the words.
Miss J. Aldrin
No fricking way!

"Would you like to see your new office?"

"This? Up here?"

"Of course. Shall we take a look?"

"Yes of course…… but then I really need to get something to eat. The nerves must have sped up my metabolism or something."

"I have a table booked…. I thought we could maybe eat together?"

She hadn't been expecting it. It caught her off guard. The thought of being alone with him over lunch, outside the office. It would be the perfect opportunity if she could manage to get the words to come out her mouth.

"Yes!" She said a little too eagerly. She was sure she heard Rebecca giggle behind them.

"That sounds lovely, thank you." She added quickly to try and regain some composure.

"Excellent, well here you are then." He pointed once more towards the door.

Once inside she was completely blown away. Unlike her other office she had heaps of space. It wasn't anywhere near as big as his but it was still a decent size. It'd been painted white to cover up the masculine wood that seemed to have been favoured in this part of the building and she could make out the scent of paint, so she knew this had all been done for her last night. It made her smile that he'd gone to so much trouble for her especially in such a short space of time. Beautiful artwork had been hung on the walls too, the bright and colourful stuff she adored.

Then there was that view. She never would have even dreamed of owning an office like this, she'd always thought she would be stuck in her little office in Covent Garden. The rent on that alone was almost as much as her flat so she knew she'd never really be able to afford to move.

There were fresh flowers in vases all around the room and the fragrant scents they gave off were filling her nostrils with varying sweet aromas. On the desk lay a brown parcel with a card on top. She'd been sure it was from him so was shocked when she turned it over.

Good luck on your first day Jane, you will be awesome. I love you! Libby xxx

Ripping the parcel open she found a framed picture of her and Libby on one of their nights out, both of them looked happy, without a care in the world. Putting it pride of place on her new desk, she turned to Andrew. She knew he must have had a part to play in this and in that moment she fell for him all over again, only harder and faster than she ever thought possible.

"Thank you..for all of this...I..." She couldn't finish her sentence, she knew she had to get him out the office and tell him. She was running on her emotions and seeing Libby's smiling face on the photograph had given her the courage she'd been searching for all morning to tell him.

"Let's go to lunch." It was as if he'd read her mind.
This was it.

She was going to finally lay her heart on the line. She hoped the next time she was back in her office it would still be in one piece and not shattered beyond repair.

~

Sitting in the restaurant a short while later, she couldn't find the words to begin bringing the subject up. She couldn't just blurt it out but at the rate this was going, that might be the only way. Seizing the chance at the first pause in conversation she clumsily blurted out.

"Andrew…there is something I need to tell you."

Oh god, oh god, oh god! She'd started so she had to go on!

"Jane? Are you ok? You're shaking!"

Her words were lost. She was staring into his eyes and knew they were stopping her brain from sending them to her mouth. Closing her eyes she whispered the words she'd never spoken to anyone but her parents or Libby before.

"Andrew..I think I am….." She trailed off. This was going to be harder than she thought.

"Wait I know I am….." *Shit, shit shit!!!!*

"Andrew.. I'm in love with you!"

Silence.

She was aware she still had her eyes closed but was too scared to open them for fear of what his face might portray, or worse he might have scarpered and left her there sitting with her eyes closed like a total imbecile. It wasn't until she felt the warmth of a hand covering her own that she dared to open them.

He was smiling at her.

Smiling!

Well that's a good start. He looked relaxed, more relaxed than he'd done all morning in fact. More relaxed than she'd ever seen him for that matter. He was gazing deeply into her eyes and she swore she could see a glint in them as his smile grew wider.

"You have no idea how pleased I am to hear you say that!"

CHAPTER 29

Andrew couldn't be sure of the exact moment he'd decided he was going to put aside all his fears and see where things went with her. All morning he'd been looking for the right moment to broach the subject, believing that it might never happen, especially while they were in work, he knew he had to get her alone. The mention of lunch was his first opportunity. It was one of the only times he could remember when he was actually glad to be so well known, it meant he could wangle a table in a top notch restaurant without a prior reservation.

Having only ever declared his love for his bitch ex-wife he knew he was out of practice and as their time at lunch was short, he'd been racking his brains for how to tell her. Then she'd gone and beaten him to it.

Hearing the words told him he'd made the right decision and knew this could be the start of something amazing.

"You are?" She looked at him as if he was joking.

"But I thought??"

"Jane I don't have a good track record with women. I usually end up hurting them, unintentionally of course and I just couldn't face doing that to you."

"Then don't!" There was a wry smile etched on her face and a testing look in her eyes.

"I will do my best, but I have to be truly honest with you before we start anything."

"What?" Now she looked worried. *Shit,* he hadn't meant to make her worry. *She just has to know a few things before this gets started.*

"Nothing serious, please don't look at me like that! I don't want to see that look on your beautiful face ever again! It's just that I work a lot so there won't always be time for..for you and me. That's the reason my relationships fail. Work will always come first and most women can't understand that."

She is smiling, thank God. He began to wonder what she could be smiling about, he'd basically just told her he would barely have time for their relationship, *does she not understand?*

"Well seeing as I work right next door to you I don't think we will have much of a problem there do you?"

Then it hit him. She was right. They would see each other every day. Together they could build an empire, do what they wanted and when.

This was perfect!

He knew in that moment that she was the one. After years of doubting he would ever be able to commit again he was now able to give away the part of him he hadn't been able to give to anyone since Carol screwed him up so badly. Yes it was scary as hell, and he wasn't one to scare easily, but he knew this felt right.

She felt right.

He made a promise to himself that he would not screw this up. Deep down he knew he wouldn't.

2 Years Later;

"Rebecca can you organise the meeting with George and Hilary for 1pm?" Jane buzzed through to her assistant.

"Of course Miss Aldrin."

Knock knock

Andrew's head peered around the door wearing a huge grin.

"Sooo, have you done it yet?"

"I have been busy working. I've had to work my arse off since you made me partner in this place." She'd loved all the extra responsibility really. He'd been so impressed with her work and their relationship had grown from strength to strength, it'd been the perfect gift for their first anniversary. Half of his business.

Okay, so to some being given a business was the least romantic gesture anyone could have made, but to her she knew he'd given her more than just a business, he'd given her his everything. His promise that she would be part of his life forever.

The re-vamped Love Games, now known as Signature of Love, was huge, bigger than she could ever have anticipated it getting. She had a whole team of people working on the floor below in charge of the day to day running. She now only dealt with the big clients, she believed, like Andrew, that the personal touch always made a difference with the big spenders. It also meant they could charge more for the service.

"All work and no play…"

"Says the biggest workaholic I know!"

"And love?"

"You know I do." And with that he walked over to her desk and kissed her hard. He'd never been the spontaneous type but since fully giving himself to her he found he just couldn't help himself around her. She was quite frequently disturbed working away in her office with his charming grin and wandering hands, and today was going to be no exception.

As the kiss grew more passionate she felt the familiar tingling sensation between her thighs. She'd grown so accustomed to feeling it whenever he was near. With this kind of kiss, it was obvious what he was after.

"Andrew, I have work to do."

He was kissing her neck and she couldn't help but close her eyes, enjoying the sweet sensations of his lips on her skin. She'd never been able to resist him but they always enjoyed playing their little games. It spurred them on, kept the heat burning. The more she resisted, the more he seemed to want her.

"You're the boss, you can take a few minutes can't you baby?" He whispered into her ear.

He was staring into her eyes. He did it on purpose, knowing the effect his ice blue eyes had on her. He used them to his advantage all the time.

She cupped his face and kissed him back. She wanted him, she always wanted him, and she couldn't deny her urges any longer. Tugging at his waistcoat and tie as if her life depended upon removing them from his body, he noticed the urgency of her moves and became more aroused.

Biting her bottom lip she unzipped his trousers, releasing him, he groaned, enjoying the freedom. The mere sight of him drove her wild.

Looking at him with a glint in her eye, she flashed her teeth and went down on him, knowing exactly how he liked it.

She knew when he was getting close and stopped. Running her hand towards the buttons of her blouse she began slowly, seductively popping each one open revealing her ample bosom, cupped by a lace bra. She could feel the tightness of her nipples trying to break free from their lacy restraint.

Andrew hastily slid a hand round her back and expertly unfastened it one handed, a trick she never tired of him performing. She loved the fact that there was none of the clumsiness she'd experienced with other men before. Throwing her head back as the pleasure took over, he started rolling her nipples between his finger and thumb. She couldn't sit still, she was desperate for him…and he knew it. He would want her to beg for him and as much as she fought it she knew that's exactly what she would end up doing….

~

When their play time had finished, she sat wrapped in his embrace, just savouring their moment together before the reality of life kicked back in and they would have to get back to work. Something they always did after they were intimate as you never knew when it could be the last time. They were both so used to things always going wrong that they were never fully able to believe this was going to be forever, despite the huge diamond that now sat pride of place on her left hand.
Beep, Beep
It was her computer telling her she had an incoming Skype call.

Quickly checking who it was she jumped up and hit answer. It was Libby and she'd been waiting for this call all morning. Pushing Andrew out of her chair, she positioned the camera properly so her best friend didn't see more than she needed.

"Get up, you told me to speak to her, so go and get dressed." He laughed but slowly did as he was told.

"Libby!!" She beamed at the monitor.

"Heya, sorry it's taken me so long, I have been mega busy."

"Well I am glad you found the time to fit me in, how's it all going?"

"Better than ever, they even talked about me taking on some interns. You look flushed, is everything ok?"

"Oh yeah, just another normal day at the office…" She flashed a grin over towards Andrew who was now fully clothed and working his way towards the door. He motioned that he was going for coffee and tapped his watch to remind her they had a client meeting shortly. She was going to have to keep this short and sweet.

"Libby, I wanted to speak to you. I have something I need to ask you…."

"I'm listening…." She obviously wasn't as Jane could clearly see her attention was on something else beside her computer screen and was only half into the conversation.

"I need you to design me a wedding dress!"
Silence

"Libby?"
Still nothing. Jane checked that the signal hadn't dropped out.
No, full signal.

"Libby??"

"Ddd..did you just say wedding dress?" She nodded at the screen, there came a loud scream of delight from the now unfrozen Libby on the other end.

"OH MY GOD!!!!! When, how?? I want all the details!"

"Well I don't have time to go into it all now Hun as I have a busy job too remember! But he asked me last night and obviously I said yes…" Holding her hand up to her face so that she could see the rock he'd given her as token of his love. Libby looked like she was going to faint.

"Jesus Jane, what size is that sexy beast?"

"Apparently it's a two carat princess cut. It's certificated and everything which i'm told is pretty good. Now I don't really know much about diamonds, but this bad boy is apparently the best you can get, a DIF or something like that. It means its basically clear and internally flawless, just like me. He went to Hatton Garden and picked it out himself." Jane was beaming. She still hadn't gotten used to the extra weight on her left hand and each time she glanced down at it she had the instant reaction of a smile.

"WOW! That is just the best news ever. It would be my honour to design your dress but you are going to need to get your arse over to Paris once in a while and bring that fine man of yours too. If he's going to be family I need to get to know him a bit better."

Jane knew she was going to have to make more of an effort to see her, but it was going to be so hard with them all having intense jobs. It made it highly unlikely they were *all* going to be in the same place at the same time.

"There is something else."

"Shit, are you pregnant? I thought you had a glow!" Jane blushed but ignored the comment.

"Would you be my maid of honour?"

"YEEEESSSSS!!!!!!" Another scream of pleasure and she couldn't be sure but was almost positive she'd detected some tears as well.

Ring Ring

The intercom.

Their clients had arrived. She knew she needed to wrap this up.

Quickly saying bye to Libby and promising to catch up with her and fill her in properly on everything, she looked up to see Andrew by the door.

"Jenny and Carl are here sweetie, are you ready?"

Looking down once more at her engagement ring and then back up to her man, she realised how much she wanted their future together. The highs and lows they would no doubt have, the good times and the bad, as long as they were together they could do anything. Together they were unstoppable and she made a vow that she wouldn't let anything come between them.

Standing up and smoothing her skirt, her hand hovered over her swollen stomach for a few of seconds longer than necessary. Flashing him her devilish smile, she'd tell him her good news later.

"Let's do this!" And she sauntered out of the office to begin their happy ending.

THE END.

COMING SOON

Finding Love: Book 2 of the Love Games Series

&

The Long Road Back

ABOUT THE AUTHOR

Laura was born in Coventry in the October of 1986 and moved to the small town of Nuneaton shortly before her first birthday. After marrying the man of her dreams in 2012 she made the big move and relocated to the South Coast where she now resides with her husband, son, noisy doggy and two cats.

When she was younger she would always be found with her nose stuck in a book, escaping the realities of the 'real world'. It has always been a dream of hers to have her work published but always ran into the same problem of never being able to finish anything she started. Life and lack of self esteem always had a knack of getting in the way.

After having her son, her whole outlook on life changed and opting to stay at home to raise him meant she had more time to dedicate to her writing too. Laura hopes that you enjoy reading her work as much as she has enjoyed writing it.

There is not usually much spare time left after looking after Charlie, doing her writing and holding down a part time job working with children, but on the odd occasion she does have some, she loves anything related to crafting. She loves to be able to see something created out of nothing, it always makes her happy and gives her a feeling of great satisfaction.

Follow me on Facebook; www.facebook.com/lauraApinks

Made in the USA
Charleston, SC
09 May 2016